Military Ethics and the Changing Nature of Warfare

International Studies on Military Ethics

THE SERIES IS EDITED UNDER THE AUSPICES OF THE INTERNATIONAL SOCIETY FOR MILITARY ETHICS IN EUROPE (EUROISME)

VOLUME 11

The titles published in this series are listed at *brill.com/isme*

Military Ethics and the Changing Nature of Warfare

Edited by

Jean-François Caron and Marina Miron

BRILL | NIJHOFF

LEIDEN | BOSTON

Cover illustration: Russian invasion in Ukraine (15 January 2023). A soldier walks by a residential building destroyed by the war in the town of Lyman. The town of Lyman liberated 3 months ago by the Ukrainian armed forces bears witness to the barbarity of war. Houses and buildings completely destroyed and civilians trying to survive (photo by Ximena Borrazas / SOPA Images/Sipa USA).

The Library of Congress Cataloging-in-Publication Data is available online at https://catalog.loc.gov
LC record available at https://lccn.loc.gov/2023013303

Typeface for the Latin, Greek, and Cyrillic scripts: "Brill". See and download: brill.com/brill-typeface.

ISSN 2214-7926
ISBN 978-90-04-54430-7 (hardback)
ISBN 978-90-04-54431-4 (e-book)

This book is printed on acid-free paper and produced in a sustainable manner.

Printed by Printforce, the Netherlands

Contents

Figures

Notes on Contributors

Jovan Babić
is Professor of Ethics at Belgrade University. He authored and edited several books and many journal articles. He is a cofounder of the International Law and Ethics Conference Series (ILECS), editor of the "Applied Ethics" series with the publishing house „Službeni glasnik" (Belgrade), a member of the BoD of EuroISME and their book series "International Studies on Military Ethics" (with Brill Nijhoff). His research interests include Kantian Ethics, Applied ethics (particularly Business Ethics, Bioethics, International Ethics, Ethics of War), and Social Ontology.

Jean-François Caron
is Associate Professor in the Department of Political Science and International Relations at Nazarbayev University where he teaches Political Theory.

Didier Danet
is a senior lecturer in the French Military Academy of Saint-Cyr. He holds a PhD in Management Sciences from the University of Rennes 1. His research interests are focusing on the changing characters of war, especially operations in the digital world, military robotics and Leadership. He is the Director of the Post Master Degree "Cyberdefense and Intangible Fields".

Gérard de Boisboissel
is a research engineer at the Saint-Cyr Military Academy Research Center (CREC Saint-Cyr), and head of the observatory *"Challenges of Emerging Technologies in the Armed Forces"*. He is in charge of coordinating research programs, specifically the programs "robotization of the battlefield" and "enhanced soldier". Heorganizes field tests with military cadets and prospectively analyzes the impact of these technologies on military uses.

Andrea Ellner
PhD (Free University, Berlin), lectures in the Defence Studies Department, King's College London. Combining historical and contemporary dimensions of military-society-government relations, she specialises on gender, armed forces and conflict, and military ethics and moral injury. She is a member of the Board of Directors of Euro-ISME and the Core Team (Gender) of the King's Centre for Military Ethics. Recent publications ‚Ein weiter Weg zum Frieden in der Ukraine – Welche Rollen für Frauen?' Positionen, *zebis*, 1 July 2022 and 'Gender

Diversity & Inclusion in Armed Forces – Ethical Perspectives on Operational Effectiveness' *Ethik und Militär* 2022/1.

David William Mac Gillavry
is an assistant professor at the Department of Leadership (Faculty of Military Leadership, Czech University of Defence), where he teaches on stress and resilience, the cognitive science of leadership, and military ethics. His research is primarily geared towards the evolutionary, cognitive and physiological foundations of human behaviour under extreme conditions and involves both laboratory and field experiments.

Zdeněk Mikulka
works as a group leader at the Department of Leadership at the University of Defence in Brno and as a lecturer at the Humanities Centre at Newton University in Brno and Prague. He specializes in applied ethics (military, security, managerial, economic and institutional), with a focus on ethical education, ethical leadership and management, and the issue of bellum iustum, and publishes regularly in these fields. Zdeněk is a former military chaplain, who has been deployed to both Kosovo and Afghanistan.

Marina Miron
PhD (2019), is a post-doctoral researcher at the Defence Studies Department, King's College London (UK) and a researcher in military science at the Colombian War College "General Rafael Reyes Prieto" (Bogota, Colombia). She has published a number of articles and chapters on ethics of cyberwarfare and terrorism.

Dragan Stanar
is Associate Professor of Military Ethics and Moral at the Military Academy of the University of Defence in Belgrade. He teaches Military Moral at the School of National Defense of the University of Defence in Belgrade and Ethics of International Politics at the Faculty of International Politics and Security. He is an elected member of the EuroISME Board of Directors. Published three books and more than 50 scientific papers on military ethics and ethics of international politics. He is also the editor-in-chief of the Ethics of Peace and War collection and a reserve officer in the Serbian Armed Forces.

Loránd Ujházi
is Professor of the Pazmany Péter Catholic University, Canon Law Institute, and Head of the Institute, Eötvös József Research Centre, Resaerch Institute for Religion and Society, University of Public Service.

Introduction

The current character of war has rapidly changed from what came to be known as hybrid warfare or sub-threshold warfare to peer-state warfare. During the previous decade both academic and military writings focused on how to counter so-called asymmetric threats emanating both from state as well as violent non-state actors (including terrorist and insurgent groups). After Russia's launch of its 'special military operation' in Ukraine in February 2022, however, both public and military discourses have shifted once again. Here one has witnessed two states facing one another on a battlefield, with one of them pursuing tactics akin to those used in the Second World War. Despite this radical shift, both sides resorted to the use of modern technologies, including cyber 'weapons', different classes of unmanned aerial vehicles, high-precision missiles and of thermobaric weapons just to name but a few. Western militaries, too, have been reacting to the technological advancements, heavily investing into development of artificial intelligence-based systems (such as the U.S. Joint All Domain Concept or JDAC) and human augmentation technologies for military personnel. These new developments – including those already in use as well as those still in development – raise a multitude of ethical questions which could not have been anticipated before, but which require timely responses.

Legal and moral norms, therefore, must shoulder the heavy burden of offering frameworks and answers to questions which simply cannot be always regulated by law. This is where military ethics finds its place by way of thinking about how the existing moral rules of warfare – otherwise known as international humanitarian law (IHL)[1] or law of armed conflict (LOAC) – ought to regulate States' and individuals' conduct during an armed conflict as to minimize suffering and protect those not taking part in the conflict.

While academic literature is replete with writings on military ethics, these are often considered from a mere theoretical perspective and often without proper consideration of what practitioners need. However, the subject is too important to be left to academics. This is where the European Society for Military Ethics (Euro-ISME) comes in. With its annual conferences dedicated to the subject, the Euro-ISME seeks to create a forum for academics, lawyers and practitioners alike where contemporary ethical challenges and emerging ethical questions can be discussed by all stakeholders. The synthesis of these

1 See Int'l Comm. Red Cross (2004), *What Is International Humanitarian Law?* retrieved from: https://www.icrc.org/eng/assets/files/other/what_is_ihl.pdf.

 | DOI:10.1163/9789004544314_002

discussions which are based on presentation by select speakers serve as a basis of this year's Euro-ISME's volume on military ethics.

The volume consists of eight chapters which focus on contemporary ethical challenges ranging from emerging military technologies to questions related to data privacy and informed consent, military ethics and ecology, military cultures as well as how the Catholic Church views war ethics. In the first chapter, Professor of Ethics at the University of Belgrade, Jovan Babić, sets the stage by looking at the changes in the character of war and how these impact military ethics. The second chapter written by Didier Danet from the Saint-Cyr Military Academy deals with a very extensive topic related to lethal autonomous weapons systems – otherwise known as 'killer robots' – and how ethical principles and legal provisions can be reconciled with considering the development and the use of such systems. To take the abstraction even further, Gérard de Boisboissel from the Saint-Cyr Military Academe analyses the issues associated with the concept of 'enhanced soldier' which entails some form of human augmentation applied to military personnel and how this idea collides with ethical approval of such 'ethical soldiers' and what ethical boundaries currently exist in the European Union when it comes to human augmentation. Associate Professor Dr Jean-François Caron from Nazarbayev University inquires into emerging ethical issues associated with informed consent related to integration of capacity-increasing technologies. David William Mac Gillavry and Dr Zdeněk Mikulka from the Defence University of Brno offer a balanced examination of the difficulties to reconcile privacy which needs to be safeguarded during recruitment data-collection and excellence, namely, the tactical and operational outputs of military missions in the 21st century. Indeed, often the respect for privacy can undermine the collection the kinds of data important to ensure mission success which presents an ethical dilemma. In the final part, Dr Dragan Stanar, associate professor at the Military Academy in Belgrade, looks at the impact of contemporary wars on environment and the inadequate treatment of this topic by the existing Just War Theory. The focus here is on ecology and how it is affected as a long-term consequence of military operations, offering a way to expand the existing theory to include this important element. Further, Dr Andrea Ellner from the Defence Studies Department at King's College London concludes the present volume with her chapter in which she examines the presence of right-wing extremist influence in military cultures and how this endangers diversity within the armed forces and what military ethics should do about this growing threat. Lastly, Loránd Ujházi, Professor of the Pazmany Péter Catholic University, examines the Catholic Church's assumptions that the idea and tradition of just war must be reconsidered in light of the imperative to protect the environment.

Overall, this volume offers a collection of topics relevant to today's military operations by focusing on topics relevant to the operational success as well as protection of the Armed Forces as well as ensuring that contemporary military operations aim beyond their immediate outputs safeguarding future stability and ensuring a lasting peace.

Jean-François Caron and Marina Miron
December 2022

CHAPTER 1

Military Ethics and War: What Is Changing and What Remains the Same?

Jovan Babić

1 Introduction

War spirit rides again! Should that be taken as a surprise? *Are* we surprised? Do we think that what has been happening now is something that had never happened before? Do we think that some other people, in the past, were not surprised in similar situations, or at least not in the same way and to the same extent as we do now? All these questions have direct relevance in the context of the theme of EuroISME's 11th conference.[1] We might have a feeling that this is different. Is it?

We can remember a rather different kind of surprise after collapse of the USSR and the end of the "Cold War" – such a big change on the global scale went without much ado, without big visible actions of what perhaps was expected: a public manifestation of victory. Victory was there, but somehow as in incomplete and unconsumed form. Has the victory of Cold War remained unconsumed, perhaps until now? Does this make the situation we have now, the pandemics, the end of "Afghanistan", and finally this war in Ukraine, different in comparison to previous wars and situations of political crises and catastrophes?

My main thesis in this short text will be that the nature of war does not change, but its perception and the attitude toward it can change, even radically. It is the same with Military Ethics.

What has changed, indeed, is the world in which we live. The world is not the same as it was recently, although the nexus of causes of everything happening now is longer, sometimes much longer, than the word "recently" may cover. On one side we have enormous technological change in our time, a change that might be compared with the changes after "discovery" of wheel,

---

1 An abridged version of this text was delivered as the Inaugural Address at the 11th EuroISME Conference "Is military ethics keeping pace with the changing character of warfare?", Budapest, May 18, 2022.

 | DOI:10.1163/9789004544314_003

or even fire. However, the changes we might perceive as the most perplexing are those occurring on a social, political, and civilizational level. Somehow, we take the world, the political world, that we have had for previous several decades, as the paradigm of normality and as the frame in which the world should and must be articulated – having its causes in clear parameters of key events we take for signs of entering in this era of normality, parameters in certain events, places and years which have a constitutive role for us in the process of articulating the life, individual and collective. We might have the feeling that the causes, and the reasons, for some of the most important changes in the world we face now originate from the year 1989 which marked the beginning of a fast end of "Cold War" (the year of Berlin Wall demolition). But what happened then has also its causes in the time prior to that year, not only 1945 but also in some previous years, most notably 1918 (the end of the first part of 20th century's world wars), 1917 (the beginning of communist experiment in Russia), 1914 (the end of the international – "European" – order established at Vienna Congress 1814),[2] and, in the distance, 1789 and 1648. Those are the years that determine the paradigm of life we live in now. The world did not begin to exist yesterday. Causes have their own causes, and although we might adore simplifications, which are mentally very comfortable and often irresistible, they cannot replace serious investigation into the complexity of all relevant causes if we sincerely and seriously want to understand, and explain, what we deem important.

Anyway, although causes work slowly, the changes sometimes come at an astonishing speed. Now seems to be one of such moments. It is obvious that the world conspicuously is not what it was only 2 years, or even 6 months, ago. Deep causes coming from the dark and forgotten or never really known or understood past triggering what now has started to evolve are very complex and, possibly, undetermined (or even undeterminable) in what their consequences are now and, especially, what they finally will be. One thing seems probable to me, and that is that the current battle of narratives might radically change to the point of unrecognizability by the end, which, the end, might be very far in the future. Sometimes I think that we are at the beginning of a new

2 The paradigm of idyllic world created at Vienna Congress 1814 collapsed after exactly hundred years, 1914. After two episodes of world wars, ending in 1945, we have two distinctly disparate world paradigm, the one established after 1945 in the context of perhaps not really finished 20th century's world wars (the time of Cold War), and the other followed the end of the Cold War. The descriptions of these two apparently short-lived paradigms are quite different from each other. They are though similar in one aspect – both were significantly shorter from the one established in Vienna 1814, in the aftermath of 1789.

"Peloponnesian War" (which lasted more than 20 years!). It might seem that those deep causes that started what has now become possible could produce many long-lasting consequences.

When we started to think and talk about what should be the theme of EuroISME's 11th conference – and that was some three years ago, immediately after we determined that the topic for the 10th conference will be "Urban Warfare" (cities always were, as they are now, key space in wars), to be held in Berlin in May 2020, on the 75th anniversary of the end of WWII – we hardly could imagine three big events that will shake our perceptions about the very essence of the subject of Military Ethics and the theme of our conference 2022: What is changing and what remains the same in the relationship between warfare and military ethics. Those three mutually very different but all huge events were the following:

1. In an indirect way, the Covid-19 pandemic, and then,
2. Quite directly, the complete withdrawal of Western presence in Afghanistan (and the return in power of the Taliban), and,
3. The Russian invasion of, or in, Ukraine.

Although the last two have directly involved huge engagement of armed forces they both are suspicious in their designation as "war". "Afghanistan" was designed at first as a punitive action after Taliban regime in Kabul rejected US request to deliver those responsible for attacks on the Twin Towers in New York on September 11th 2001, and then gradually became a long-term military engagement still not easy interpretable as "war" – until its rather strange abrupt ending 20 years later. Regarding the Russian invasion in Ukraine, a part of the "battle of narratives" (to which I will return shortly) is "waged" precisely over the words suitable to name it: Russians proclaimed it to be a "special military operation", while the West promptly designated it as an act of aggression. In neither case it is not clear if it is a regular *war*. I will elaborate a bit on that later too, trying to show how complicated is the web of its causes and how immense is the scope of possibilities that might evolve from that event, which opens the room for too many radically different interpretations: from its being an act of aggressive and reckless breaking of international law and order, irresponsible attack on another country, act of revenge and fear, or yet as a "military intervention" (in Russian view even humanitarian in its nature), to "punitive action", to hidden civil war, to some even more complicated schemes like the one implying its religious roots or civilizational ramifications. The plausibility of any of these interpretations will depend on what will happen in the future, possibly the farther future. It is strange and hard to bear this idea that future should have such counter-causal impact.[3] Part of our discontent certainly comes from this, not only in the way in which uncertainty produces nervousness and discomfort. But we also might sense a kind of arrogance in the assumption that the future is not open but determined in advance.

All this talk about interpretations might appear as a semantic matter and not of real significance, but it is of direct relevance for the topic of our conference: Has the concept of war changed, and in what sense and direction? However, this also is not a new problem – it is something we have had with many, if not most, armed conflicts from 1945 (but also for many before), always producing perplexity on what it is about, *war or something else*. Military interventions always tend to be interpreted as police actions (and many American soldiers engaged in Iraq or Afghanistan were saying "action" rather than "war" – as if it will be easier for their wives, mothers, and families to endure their absence, taking "war" to be something much more dangerous and latently wrong). But, as Michael Walzer writes – in the Introduction to his fabulous short book *Arguing About War,*– "we can't change reality by changing the way we talk about it, as we can see in the original case: The UN police action in Korea in 1950 is called a war by all historians" (Walzer, 2005, p. XIII–XIV). Is it – only – the magnitude of that particular "action" (or its duration, in Afghanistan) – that matters or is there something more specific in the definition of a particular conflict that designates it as a "war"? For example, in Korean so called "UN police action" we had "the UN air force" bomb with napalm stretch more than 200 kilometers long and 30 kilometers wide, in which all living things were burnt, all men, women, children, animals, and plants – with a purpose to cut off Chinese supply chains from behind: Can we possibly designate and name "cutting supply chains", even of less magnitude than this one, to anything short of "war"?!

2 World in a Process of Change

When we started talking about the theme for EuroISME's Budapest Conference we were motivated by quite different concerns from those that we encounter now. Also, we are now in a mood, if I may say so, regarding the context

3 This counter-causal effect will reinterpret and transform, in the future, the articulation of the present time (which then will be the past), changing our reality *ex post facto*. This obviously is very repulsive as it implies that some, possibly many, of our current beliefs and values based upon them will prove to be false and wrong.

in which we are talking now quite differently from the one we had envisaged then. I remember John Thomas[4] suggesting, in Paris, 2019, that the very definition of military ethics should be explored in terms of its facing changes we were convinced are so big that they might change the very nature and essence of human conflicts, including warfare, presuming that warfare is something on a declining line in our time, and even that conflicts should be surmountable and mastered, of course after we find the way how to control the growing development of technology that, although it sometimes seems to get out of hand, is making the regulation of life ever more efficient and better. We were tempted to even conceive that wars and massive armed conflicts are becoming obsolete and, being unnecessary, might be replaced by something like "*security management*", opening the perspectives of policing the world. The sentiments were much more optimistic than they are now.

The changes we were thinking of then were directed to questions about how to cope with technological challenges in two ways – once, firstly, in the sense of *ius in bello:* how to regulate what has not been regulated yet – new practices (drones, autonomous weapons, remote control, visibility and hiding, etc.), but also, secondly, in the sense of *ius ad bellum,* with the question if the very nature of warfare has changed so much that not only its needed articulation but its very nature becomes more controllable and avoidable. I think that John, on at least two of our BoD meetings in Paris, indicated to this second aspect of what is possibly new in our dealing with warfare. I will later return briefly to the issue of *ius ad bellum* because its understanding, or the lack thereof, is the source of some misunderstandings in our approach to the phenomenon of war – not its bad regulation but our one-sided and distorted perception of what leads to decisions upon which wars start, and how they might become unavoidable because of that. It is not the lack of regulation, or bad articulation of the regulation of the conduct of warfare, but it is our understanding that the very nature of those three events we faced in the meantime made us believe that we are witnessing something that is not only unexpected but also something that, according to those optimistic sentiments, shouldn't happen at all.

[There is an interesting question here regarding how much our obsession with the so called "Just War Theory" (JWT), with its far-reaching Manichean implications and idolatry of our perceiving ourselves as striving for "perfection" and "justice" independently of really existing interests of real people, is what prevents us from understanding the deeper logic of human agency and the need for coordination and cooperation within it – not only to be morally right but also to be functionable and sustainable].

4 President of EuroISME.

But at that moment then, three years ago, we wanted to explore if the nature of warfare had changed "paradigmatically": do we have a change of the very paradigm of it. The normative aspect, or content, of that change might have been perceived very differently – for example some apparently perceived and took drones, and the enhanced precision on the operational level, as a betterment because the ratio of death and damage might decrease, while others perceived the same as worsening and even evil because it reduces personal experience which, according to that approach, has a dehumanizing effect and transforms engagement in war into something rather mechanical and impersonal, something we can be indifferent to, destroying those feelings upon which we base our conception of attributability of responsibility for what we do. It is much more than the issue of regulating warfare (which is the domain of *ius in bello*, and which depends in great part on prevailing and accepted sensitivities at a particular time – presuming that we are very sensitive).

It is strictly an issue of *ius ad bellum:* does perceived change of the paradigm of warfare require change in the scope of justifying war as such, or even disallows it entirely independently of any regulation? Something seems to be lost there. For example, the intimacy of war, and of battle, is not only a condition for the virtues of warriors but also the condition of its human permissibility (preserving some respect to others and to oneself, the respect and care for those whom we might endanger or kill in the process of maintaining the business of war). It might seem that impersonal character of modern warfare, through the dehumanization it implies, makes participating in such inhuman practice senseless and unacceptable. If modern warfare excludes any confrontation with the enemy, if it reduces the enemy to something like insects, or like hunting targets, the nature of war might be seen as changed, and to the extent to which our perception determines what is the reality of what we can do it changes the very nature of what we are doing then. Hunting and warring are not, and should not be, or taken to be, as same. It reduces persons to mere means, something that persons rightly or wrongly should not be reduced to. The very difference between right and wrong would be lost.

So, we had a good theme, independently from those three big events that might change our original intent regarding our 11th Conference.

But then, in this short period of two years we faced those three events that change the whole reality as we perceived and experienced it before them occurring. These events were not the results of those changes we noticed before and took as the reason for the theme of our conference – changes brought by technology, environmental issues, or perhaps by our enhanced sensitivities which lead us to arrogantly believe that we are better than those who lived on Earth before us. On the contrary, these three events follow the same deeper logic that we may find already in Herodotus: making decisions in borderline situations. Still there is a question: Do they really change the topic of our Conference? They could be the results of some developments quite independent from what we perceived as relevant and exciting changes that lead us to formulate the topic of our conference in the way we did – and still make such an impact on us to make us refocus our attention to them from what was our focus before. As I listed them above, they are, in the order of their appearance: the Covid-19 pandemic, the withdrawal of the last US forces from Afghanistan, and the Russian invasion in Ukraine. Let me make some remarks about all of them, in that order.

3 Three Big Events, in Less Than Three Years

3.1 *Covid-19 Pandemic*

Firstly, we faced the strange situation resulting from the Covid-19 pandemic, postponing our "Berlin conference", which was eventually held online with a year of delay. That conference was successful, although it brought some unexpected experiences to us regarding its virtual character which, probably, would have not happened if it was held "in person". It happened that the consequences of this different format of last year's conference consumed a lot of our energy and time, producing even more directly the need to explore the topic of this year's one – independently of the big events we encountered as we entered the process of defining our mission and, within it, attempting to define what military ethics is now, and what we, as a professional organization, are supposed to do – how we perceive ourselves and our mission in the actual world. The pandemic itself was important for military ethics. First, it was, and was perceived as, a catastrophe, not a simple crisis. It produced an enormous amount of security concerns, but also unprecedented global solidarity (despite revealing many discrepancies within established schemes of cooperation, global and national, and even blatant cases of what might be designated as "international selfishness"). The world was united during the pandemic in a way in which perhaps it never was before. A specific feature relevant for military ethics was the obviousness that in a situation of extreme need most or all other constraints must fall back. This image of seriousness is something specific for military, more than other human activities, and armies around the world followed the demands of that seriousness very thoroughly and better than any other part of human societies and its structural parts (shown in confusions and misunderstandings of what "rights", civil, individual, and other, are possibly imperiled, producing very obscure anti-vaccination movement). The logic of necessity unveiled in the pandemic was of the same type as that present in the logic on which we base feelings of emergency latently always present in the military and their vigilance and readiness to engage at any moment. These feelings are reflected in the impression of importance of military ethics, indicating that continuity of life is a supreme commandment, even when it comes into collision with accumulated rights and established expectations that, perhaps, to some extent have spoiled the humankind. In the context of huge progress in knowledge, wealth, and well-being, surpassing any previous epoch, the global pandemic was confined in a much more comfortable version of "quarantine" than ever before.

3.2 *Afghanistan*

Second, Afghanistan – it came to most of us as a surprise, but it is interesting to understand why? One of the questions raised was if a professional association dealing with military ethics has any possible role in facilitating or preventing such "evils" as "the catastrophe of the Fall of Kabul". I am inclined to say both "No" and "Yes" here: "No", it is not the business of military ethicists to behave like activists, even in the weak sense of the word "activism" that might be applied, for example, to the activities of Red Cross (who also are not activists, in the sense in which participants in warfare, or pacifists, or other partisans, are). "Yes", in the sense that part of our mission is to help in proper interpretation of what happened in "Kabul", demonstrating that it was not a "catastrophe" and not even a "defeat" but a logical and even belated decision that might even be recognized as an example of "imperial wisdom". Should Americans and their allies have stayed there forever?

"Afghanistan" is ethically interesting and relevant for several reasons. One is the speed of withdrawal for successful military interventions aspiring to be justified: should such interventions be quick? It was the case with three such events which in literature are almost universally uncontested: India's intervention in East Pakistan, when Bangladesh was born, Tanzania's in Uganda, when the sinister dictatorship of Idi Amin was abolished, and Vietnam's in Kampuchea (before and now known as Cambodia), when Paul Pot's regime was pushed back into the jungle.

The second is the relation between justification of entering and exiting: it might be easy to enter and start but difficult to finish and exit. Unlike Iraq, where such justification is absent in both aspects, in Afghanistan might be the opposite: while in Iraq there was no proper justification for "entering" (WMD were never found), Afghanistan was different – it's not easy to reject that some strong justification for it was present then in the Fall of 2001. The justification to exit was achieved rather soon, and certainly after the so called "war on terror" was relocated, or when Al Qaeda lost its monopolistic role therein. There were at least two such moments: after killing Bin Laden, and after the American engagement against ISIL began.

What is interesting from the ethical point of view is that in Iraq there was no proper justification for leaving also, which might indicate how the situations might be complex and hard to discern: the fact that intervention was unjustified doesn't imply that you are automatically justified to leave. In the meantime, there were consequences produced by the intervention and those consequences might be a matter of direct responsibility for the intervener – in this case the result of leaving was leaving civilians unprotected, the rise of ISIL, and destruction of Mosul was just one of the consequences. There is an interesting comparison in a paper[5] by David Rodin: the fact that we unjustifiably (or accidentally) have "dangled" somebody out of the window does not imply that we have a right to allow them to fall: we might *have a duty* to hold them as firmly and as long as we can to prevent the disaster of them falling down. So, while the exiting Afghanistan might be an example of "imperial wisdom", it is not easy to say the same for Iraq. I may be wrong here but the only issue for me is why the West did not leave earlier? However, they were justified in both, entering and exiting, and the "Fall of Kabul" was not a moral catastrophe (nor a serious defeat of the West, certainly not comparable with "Vietnam"). You have not to be a cultural relativist to admit that.

3.3 *Ukraine*

The third of three big events that made a change in the atmosphere we are experiencing now is the most complex, the most obscure and possibly the most significant of the three. Russian invasion of Ukraine is a game changing event. It would be such even if Russians succeeded in their alleged original intent – to promptly bring Ukraine to order after years long provocations and bad and undetermined internal and international realities in those areas, and will be such even if Russia were defeated – this is discernible from the fact that now it is becoming a matter that has less and less connection with direct causes of the conflict, acquiring features of what I labeled at the beginning as *a*

5 Rodin, 2015, p. 687: "Suppose that dangling someone out a window against their will is wrong and that dangling for a longer period is morally worse than dangling for a shorter period. One day I decide to suspend you by the ankles from my twelfth-floor apartment window, just for fun. Suddenly I experience an epiphany and realize how shabbily I am treating you. But I cannot get you back through the window on my own. I will have to hope that I can hold on till my flat mate comes home in half an hour ... Although dangling you from my window is wrong, and the longer I dangle the worse it is, the one thing I morally must not do is to let go".

new "Peloponnesian war". We always knew, or at least should have known, that the most basic characteristic of wars is their *unpredictability*. Desire to avoid, or at least diminish, the impact of this parameter of unpredictability produces our efforts to devise schemes like "JWT" on the theoretical level, or schemes of "asymmetric warfare", "humanitarian interventions", or RTP, on doctrinal and ideological level. Although Russians at first started to rationalize their operation by using the vocabulary of JWT, it is rather obvious that none of the current theoretical or doctrinal schemes is satisfactory. The only thing that seems certain to me is that what's going on there cannot be reduced to a semantical or marketing level, nor to, e. g., who is louder in shouting their narrative (or more efficient in silencing their opponents, "deplatforming" them, as they say now). It cannot be settled by burning on stakes a few Giordanos Brunos. It doesn't seem fit in any available scheme. So, what is it?

Many would say now that it came as a surprise. Certainly, there were no ultimatums, but warnings were not missing, so that sometimes it seems that it was only a matter of time. It started as "a special military operation" defined in essence partly as a humanitarian intervention and partly as a punitive action (like the one in Afghanistan in the fall of 2001). But the picture is not that clear. What is it really? Is it a punitive action against "unruly Kiev regime" or pure and, as we could have heard countless times, "unprovoked aggression"? Was it a pre-emptive attack countering what was threatening either as impermissible discrimination within Ukraine against a part of their own population or was it a strategic threat to Russian security manifested in Ukraine's desire to become a member of NATO pact (which is a military alliance encircling Russia)? These are two different, partly mutually independent partly overlapping, lines of possible argumentation in this matter.

Besides, regarding the timing it may be perceived as either belated or premature, the first showing some potentially important insecurities, the second manifesting impatience to wait until when the clear *casus belli* would be more, or at all, visible to all. Was that impatience a result of despair, or just vanity and irresponsibility? Is it a "proxy war" on the part of the West, or is it more a hidden civil war evolved from who knows which accumulated causes rolled beneath deposited layers in who knows which dark past of those areas? Is it just the continuation or remnant of the Cold War, or its final ending stage, localized, perhaps only temporarily, on the part of the territory of former USSR – we may recall that USSR was a nameless state created on the territory of former Russian Empire, on the crossroads between Asia and Europe, but by not having a proper name that political structure might be anywhere (also we should not forget that communism was a sinister and far reaching– anti-Russian?, anti-European? – experiment of enormous proportions)? Is it perhaps an attempt to revise the outcome of the Cold War? Or to reestablish the main feature of the Cold War: its Manichean black and white character of "Two (opposite) Worlds", a picture which might look comfortable at first glance. Does it, or will it, have an impact on the issue if Russia is in essence "European", or not really? If not, what's her essence then (and what is the essence of "Europeanism", then and in general?)? Finally, is it quite a different kind of conflict, for example a global civilizational conflict between imperial democracy with its optimistic ideology of accumulative progress in universal happiness of unidentified individuals (construed as Nozickian pleasure-machines), on the one side, and traditional world based on in the past accumulated but in the meantime become to be felt or perceived as obsolete and backward, even reactionary, set of virtues manifested in various kinds of identities, heterogeneous and variable, on the other? Might it be some homeostatic reflex or impulse coming from some very deep but not very visible, even unknown, layer of reality indicating a cardinal crisis of humankind? The plausibility of any of these interpretations, or any of combinations thereof, will depend on what will happen in the future, possibly farther future.

A bit more on the concept of a new "Peloponnesian War". We can wonder if the apparent implausibility of such an interpretation comes only from its being cumbersome, or more from the impression of its not fitting well into accepted fashionable or ideologically correct schemes of interpretation? We can recall Thucydides' words that that (Peloponnesian) war was a product of false beliefs and even more unfounded hopes. Hope, says Thucydides, is a dangerous notion (Thucydides, 5:103). On the other hand, Hobbes says that even the weakest and most stupid may kill the strongest and smartest, by using the instrument of cunningness, which is an essential and inalienable part of the capacity of reason (Hobbes, XIII.1–2). That's the point at which the possibility of falsehood of beliefs enters the context of accepting enticing hopes, assuming that they satisfy Thucydides' requirement regarding hopes: that we should not rely on them if we do not have at our disposal "enough resources" – but resources are also a vague term. The dangerous word here is the word "enough",[6] it cannot be determined in advance.[7] And hope and belief conflate their meanings in

6 A similar argument referring to the word and notion of "enough", regarding the amount of force that is justified to be used in self-defense might be found in Narveson (1965), p. 268: as it is not determinable in advance it cannot be defined in formal and exact way (regarding the allowed amount of applicable force etc.). In military context this is the source of uncertainty in defining precise demarcation lines in issues of proportionality.

7 This is the reason why supremacy cannot take the form of *omnipotence* but has to stay at the level of (plausible) assessment of a superior strength, which entails that it is not possible to secure desired outcome with absolute certainty: unpredictability cannot be eliminated.

the belief that the other side is not only weaker but that they also know that they are weaker and that because of that they won't fight back. As we know, although Athenian imperial democracy was much stronger, economically and militarily, from Sparta, the hubris which led Athenians to rely on arrogant hope based in the feeling of omnipotence led them to the Syracusan catastrophe. The result was the destruction of one civilization, and making way for another one, perhaps not so good and sublime.

If Russia "cannot afford" to lose, and we have difficulties conceiving her winning – in whichever of three possible forms of it: either as an accepted and sustainable solution of the civil war, or as victory in the proxy war, or just as an imposed truce proclaimed to be a new peace, with all the baggage of what the consequences of one or the other would be for the world – we might get the impression of a very long-lasting conflict, the one in which the battle of narratives we are so immersed in today may be mostly forgotten, and even so the reasons that led to first decisions that triggered it all. But if the solution depends on hopeless task of getting to the position in which conflicting parties would agree to listen to each other, the perspective does look gloomy indeed: ignoring has been felt as too irresistible. The sentiments ruling over us now are efficiently preventing us to see what we perhaps will see only after much lost time (and everything else that also might be lost, perhaps forever). The unpredictability might give the full capacity of its workload then, and the flow of time might make the situation ever worse since what was not known at first, due to refusal to listen, will be even more difficult to grasp then (even in improbable case of sudden curiosity producing strong desire to explain and understand) – making agreeing on an acceptable solution be very difficult, and resulting in the impossibility to tell what the accepted paradigm of a new reality will be.

Of course, we may insist on scholastic analysing or on blaming –asking why what is happening is not as it should be. For example, we can, as my colleague Ted van Baarda and I came to in our correspondence regarding this matter, invoke the international law and say that we face a clear case of aggression by violating the article 2(4) of the UN Charter which is taken to be one of the cornerstones of international law in last decades. Or we can theorize that the Russian president got caught in a trap like that of Napoleon III, who was convinced that the wisest move he could make is to attack what was from his

The probabilistic feature of the war, as anything coming from within the scope of freedom, allows some, however small, but real, chance of failure. You cannot be sure to have "enough resources" to realize your hopes. Unlike omnipotence, superiority cannot eliminate the unpredictability, and guarantee a desired outcome.

perspective an unruly kingdom of Prussia which obviously was producing a new political reality of Europe at the time. Or we can, as sometimes it seems to me, name new evils with old names, and then be caught in the web of outdated schemes from the past. Or we can attempt to rationalize, ignore, or even justify horrible events like the one that took place in Odessa on May 2, 2014, when more than 50 people were burnt alive. Or we may on the contrary apply the principle *uti possidetis iuris* on present or recent administrative borders, drawn arbitrarily and now producing unsolvable conflicts (as we have seen in many other places in the world, where borders have strong external recognition but often no internal one based in sincere and informed consent, implying that's territory only, not peoples or living persons, what counts)? And so on.

Do we still need military ethics?

Our main question – do we still need military ethics? – received an unexpected corroboration. Military ethics is more important and needed than ever, in this time where the *normality* of *status quo ante* was taken as something obvious and at the same time is cardinally contested. What has been taken as obvious became suddenly bleak and unconvincing. Instead of normality of established peace, based in trust, confidence, and universal respect, it seems that now to many of us war looks more "normal" than peace. Military ethics has new challenges.

Our colleague in EuroISME's BoD, Patrick Mileham, has two, actually three, essential ideas regarding military ethics of utmost interest for our theme: first, that war is always a battle of narratives, second that war is a kind of experiment, a jump into unknown, that it is a matter of trying and of daring. The function of daring is, of course, a complex issue of conditions, beliefs, contexts, assumptions, prejudices, hopes, etc., but to start a war on both sides one must dare to accept that horrible rule of the game we call war. That game has its constitutive rules, and as all games has the capacity to change reality by creating new facts. (The third of Patrick's basic claims is that there is a difference between ethics and morality, a distinction to avoid so called "Is/Ought Gap", on which another distinction, that between *ius in bello* and *ius ad bellum,* is based.)

The experimental character of war shows in its feature of unpredictability, i.e., absence of any reliable control of future time. This is a direct implication of freedom as the power to make something that would not exist without free decision. Human position in the universe is characterized by two basic parameters: fallibility and vulnerability (both contributing to moral equality of all persons). Fallibility is contained even in natural science, which is empirical and based in induction, not in deduction. But in the realm of freedom it is different: there is no reliable predictability what we, and especially what others, will want and decide in future, making uncertainty contained in freedom much more cardinal than that contained in mere fallibility of knowledge as such. That makes experimental character of war very different from other, mere empirical (or scientific) experiments: the calculus of probability there is much vaguer and there is no progress in acquiring new knowledge in it. I am not sure if Patrick has thought of this aspect of experiment in his idea of war as experiment, but it seems to me that this entails a huge additional responsibility to us, as candidates to be military ethicists, in our efforts to understand, explain and evaluate any particular war. (It is much easier within *ius in bello,* the issue there being in compliance with the established rules, which, as in all laws and other conventions, could have been different but factually are not: the only problem there might be their imprecision and indeterminacy, but other than that they are just the matter to apply).

The other of Patrick's items, the "battle of narratives" is intimately connected with the previous one. Narratives are in essence the interpretations of what is happening. From our fallibility follow some difficulties to achieve an absolutely true description (every description is also an ascription!), but in a situation of conflict, which is based in freedom and additional fallibility, the business of interpreting becomes itself a matter of the conflict, more than the matter of understanding, explaining or justified evaluation of what is the subject of interpretation. And for an ethicist it might be a problem. The business of military ethics is not quite scientific: to study wars as phenomena. It is more normative: to explore their possible justifications (in the context of their *prima facie* unjustifiability). However, the process of justifying must be solid, which it cannot be if not objective and impartial. That implies, at least, not jumping to conclusions, and serious and responsible effort to find and explore causes of what is the matter of analyzing. Causes have two main features: they produce consequences, and they come from the past. Neither of these should be changed in the process of interpreting or reinterpreting. If we do that, we start a strange business of producing miracles: *only miracles are causeless,* and sometimes also reasonless. But in the context of stress, anger, rage, or resentment, it might be difficult to resist such a temptation to replace causal explanation with miraculous fairy-telling that is certainly much more comfortable. Our need to blame is also easier to satisfy that way, but that is too high price – for what? For an illusory option to be able to ascribe stupidity and evil to those whom we hate?

That might be the biggest risk, epistemological and moral: – to come to the position that our blame is based in a strange attitude that those whom we hate are because of that stupid and then, also, evil: *we don't hate them because they are stupid and evil, but they are stupid and evil because we hate them.* (This does not preclude that they might be really stupid, and also evil, but that doesn't change the starting attitude which invalidates any claim to the objectivity of such analysis). Nourishing hatred is investment in future enmity and we cannot know if that enmity wouldn't prove to be uncontrollable. But what we can know (if we wish and dare to) is that time won't stop, and that the moment of desperate need for reconciliation will certainly come, even if it will look as impossible. Such position may make any negotiation hopelessly implausible and ineffective and can preclude a sustainable reconciliation. It may lead to total war, without room for sound thinking and without responsibility.

Perhaps it is not impossible but certainly it is neither plausible nor right to be a judge in one's own affairs. You cannot take a side and be a judge at the same time. In order to stay in our lane, it is necessary not to be lost in the frenzy or hysteria of arrogant propriety, disabling us from sound thinking necessary for seriousness and responsibility in what we do, in deeds and words, especially when the issues are very important as they sometimes are. That's the only way to not only stay in our lane but also to get a chance to move forward.

CHAPTER 2

Lethal Autonomous Weapons Systems: Could Ethical Principles and Legal Provisions Be Reconciled?

Didier Danet

1 Introduction

In 2012, Human Rights Watch and Harvard University published the famous report "Losing Humanity". In the wake of this report, a campaign was initiated to call for a ban on R&D programs that could lead to the production and implementation of Lethal Autonomous Weapons Systems (LAWS), rebranded as "Killer Robots".[1] This campaign was (and still is) supported by a broad coalition of non-governmental organizations.[2] A negotiation process was initiated within the Convention on Certain Conventional Weapons (CCCW),[3] which aim is to prohibit or restrict the use of conventional weapons considered

1 Denise Garcia, 'The Case against Killer Robots: Why the United States Should Ban Them' (2014) 10 Foreign Affairs 2014; Mark Gubrud, 'Stopping Killer Robots' (2014) 70 Bulletin of the Atomic Scientists 32; Armin Krishnan, *Killer Robots: Legality and Ethicality of Autonomous Weapons* (Ashgate 2009); Noel E Sharkey, 'Saying "No!"To Lethal Autonomous Targeting' (2010) 9 Journal of Military Ethics 369; Robert Sparrow, 'Killer Robots' (2007) 24 Journal of applied philosophy 62.

2 Charli Carpenter, 'Rethinking the Political/-Science-/Fiction Nexus: Global Policy Making and the Campaign to Stop Killer Robots' (2016) 14 Perspectives on Politics 53; Rouven Tschersich, 'The Campaign to Stop Killer Robots and Its Media Problems: An Analysis of a Newspaper Discourse Surrounding a Campaign against a Malicious Technology' (BS thesis, University of Twente 2018); Gubrud (n 1); Stephen D Goose and Mary Wareham, 'The Growing International Movement against Killer Robots' (2016) 37 Harvard International Review 28.

3 M Patrick Cottrell, 'Legitimacy and Institutional Replacement: The Convention on Certain Conventional Weapons and the Emergence of the Mine Ban Treaty' (2009) 63 International Organization 217; Robert J Mathews, 'The 1980 Convention on Certain Conventional Weapons: A Useful Framework despite Earlier Disappointments' (2001) 83 International Review of the Red Cross 991; J Ashley Roach, 'Certain Conventional Weapons Convention: Arms Control or Humanitarian Law' (1984) 105 Mil. L. Rev. 3; Stephanie Carvin, 'Conventional Thinking? The 1980 Convention on Certain Conventional Weapons and the Politics of Legal Restraints on Weapons during the Cold War' (2017) 19 Journal of Cold War Studies 38.

 | DOI:10.1163/9789004544314_004

excessively injurious or whose effects are indiscriminate (non-detectable fragments, incendiary weapons, blinding laser weapons …).[4]

It took ten years to come to … almost nothing. Negotiations have been sinking in endless debates on the characterization of machine "autonomy" and the proper definition of what LAWS are.[5] Negotiators only agreed on a series of eleven principles to rule the negotiations.[6] These principles are not completely useless. Participants agree on the relevance of the CCCW arena to negotiate, which was not undisputed in the early stages of the process. More important, participants state that the making and implementation of LAWS is subject to Humanitarian Law provisions. This principle may seem obvious but its consequences are of utmost importance.[7]

The first part of the paper deals with the possible explanations and the consequences of the failure of negotiations which took place in Geneva. The aim of this first part is to establish that no legal provisions can be set without a shared definition of LAWS (which is far from being the current state of the negotiation process) However, the bogging down of the negotiations and the absence of an explicit prohibition of LAWS does not mean that arms industry or the military are free to design, develop and implement any terrifying weapons systems they would dream of. In fact, weapons systems such as LAWS are here and now regulated and prohibited, which is challenging the real use of an explicit prohibition of an arm category that no one is able to give an uncontroversial definition of.

---

4 Roach (n 3); Mathews (n 3); Malcolm Shaw, 'The United Nations Convention on Prohibitions or Restrictions on the Use of Certain Conventional Weapons, 1981' (1983) 9 Review of International Studies 109.

5 Elvira Rosert and Frank Sauer, 'How (Not) to Stop the Killer Robots: A Comparative Analysis of Humanitarian Disarmament Campaign Strategies' (2021) 42 Contemporary Security Policy 4; Deane Baker, *Should We Ban Killer Robots?* (John Wiley & Sons 2022).

6 Diego Mauri, 'Building the Bridge to the Future', *Autonomous Weapons Systems and the Protection of the Human Person* (Edward Elgar Publishing 2022); Tsvetelina van Benthem, 'The Regulation of Militarised Artificial Intelligence: Protecting Civilians through Legal Reviews of New Weapons and Precautions', *Regulating Artificial Intelligence in Industry* (Routledge 2021).

7 Ryan Poitras, 'Article 36 Weapons Reviews & Autonomous Weapons Systems: Supporting an International Review Standard' (2018) 34 Am. U. Int'l L. Rev. 465; Thompson Chengeta, 'Are Autonomous Weapons Systems the Subject of Article 36 of Additional Protocol I to the Geneva Conventions' (2016) 23 UC Davis J. Int'l L. & Pol'y 65; Charles J Dunlap Jr, 'Accountability and Autonomous Weapons: Much Ado about Nothing' (2016) 30 Temp. Int'l & Comp. LJ 63; Johin Lewis, 'The Case for Regulating Fully Autonomous Weapons' (2014) 124 Yale LJ 1309.

The second part of the paper is starting from this example of LAWS prohibition to examine the connection between Law and Ethics in relation with military innovations. Do we really need new legal provisions in order to regulate, authorize or prohibit military innovations that could infringe ethical principles? Should legal provisions explicitly ban any potential new weapons system, such as "Killer Robots"? Are we losing humanity if special laws do not define new frameworks for arms industry? In this second part, we argue that the existing set of laws is most often relevant to regulate military innovations and that not so many new provisions are really needed to preserve humanity in military conflicts.

2 Why Ethics and Law Seem to Diverge on Killer Robots?

Law and Ethics seem to stand on opposite sides as far as "Killer Robots" are concerned. Taking advantage of scientific strides and industrial innovation to build machines that decide of human beings' life and death is going against major basic principles of common Ethics.[8] However, contracting parties in the CCCW did not agree on a binding rule that would prohibit autonomous weapons systems on the battlefield. Does this mean that the law-making process is flawed et that some countries give a preference to such considerations as scientific, industrial or military gains over the preservation of ethical principles? Many supporters of the ban express this opinion. This paper emphasizes two another explanations to the failure of negotiations related to "Killer Robots" in Geneva. The first one puts forward the lack of a shared definition of what is supposed to be prohibited. What can be considered a "Lethal Autonomous Weapons System"? What are the specific features of such systems? How would it be possible to distinguish an autonomous system from a non-autonomous system or a partially autonomous system? Defining LAWS is complicated but it is a preliminary step to any prohibition or regulation legal provision. The other explanation of the failure is dealing with the usefulness of a specific prohibition of LAWS. Such bans exist under International Humanitarian Law for blinding lasers or invisible ammunition splinters (among others) Would an explicit new ban on "Killer Robots" be of great use? Is arms industry free to engage in research and development programs aiming at providing machines

---

8 Amanda Sharkey, 'Autonomous Weapons Systems, Killer Robots and Human Dignity' (2019) 21 Ethics and Information Technology 75; Noel Sharkey, 'Robotics Today : The Good, Bad and Ugly', *31 mars – 4 avril* (David W Bustard & Roy Sterrirr 2008); NE Sharkey, 'The Ethical Frontiers of Robotics' (2008) 322 Science 1800.

with the capability to make their own decisions on life and death on the battlefield? Are the military eager to benefit from such systems and their alleged advantages?

2.1 *Autonomous Lethal Weapons Systems: Looking for a Definition*

Defining ' Killer Robots ' is a tricky challenge for different reasons.[9] First, political, economic and military stakes are huge and bring pressure on the definition of what is in to be regulated. The wider the criterium of "autonomy", the bigger the number of military systems about to be banned or, at least, under scrutiny and constraining rules. Harsh debates took place in the beginning of the negotiations about unmanned aerial vehicles (such as Predator drones for example) On the one side, some NGOs considered that certain existing weapons systems were not to be excluded from the field of LAWS prohibition.[10] On the opposite, French and other governmental experts clearly stated that LAWS prohibition would only be relevant for future weapons systems. The criteria and definitions were then designed to fit with these respective goals, which did not ease conceptual clarification.

Then, defining "autonomy" and "control" in relation with a military robot is quite challenging from a conceptual and scientific point of view.[11] For most people, the best image of a LAWS is the Terminator, the famous cyborg assassin sent from the future by Skynet, a hostile artificial intelligence. As a cyborg, the Terminator looks like a man but it is, in fact, nothing more than an exoskeleton covered with artificial flesh and driven by an artificial intelligence. This representation which is very influential is however paradoxical. The Terminator is precisely all but a good example of "autonomous machine". It is designed and preprogrammed to execute one and only one single mission: tracking and

9 Ingvild Bode and Thomas Watts, 'Meaning-Less Human Control: Lessons from Air Defence Systems on Meaningful Human Control for the Debate on AWS' [2021] Centre for War Studies, University of Southern Denmark; Benjamin Kastan, 'Autonomous Weapons Systems: A Coming Legal' Singularity'?' [2013] U. Ill. JL Tech. & Pol'y 45; Ángel Gómez de Ágreda, 'Ethics of Autonomous Weapons Systems and Its Applicability to Any AI Systems' (2020) 44 Telecommunications Policy 101953.

10 Rebecca Crootof, 'The Killer Robots Are Here: Legal and Policy Implications' (2014) 36 Cardozo L. Rev. 1837; Heather M Roff, 'The Strategic Robot Problem: Lethal Autonomous Weapons in War.' (2014) 13 Journal of Military Ethics 211.

11 Bode and Watts (n 9); Michael Horowitz and Paul Scharre, 'Meaningful Human Control in Weapon Systems: A Primer' [2015] Working Paper March; Daniele Amoroso and Guglielmo Tamburrini, 'Autonomous Weapons Systems and Meaningful Human Control: Ethical and Legal Issues' (2020) 1 Current Robotics Reports 187; Merel Ekelhof, 'Moving beyond Semantics on Autonomous Weapons: Meaningful Human Control in Operation' (2019) 10 Global Policy 343.

killing Sarah Connors. It can use multiple skills and abilities to reach this goal but it did not choose to be part of the mission, does not question the legitimacy of the goal, does not experience any feelings or moral dilemma ... No suffering or pain, until total destruction, may divert the Terminator from the unique goal that was assigned to its central unit by an external authority. The Terminator is just a preprogrammed machine, which is tied to an exclusive mission that it cannot question or modify on its own initiative.

So, if the Terminator is not a good image of what a LAWS is, how to define such a system and characterize its main features? Unmanned Aerial Vehicles, namely the US Predator and Reaper drones, were in the line of sight of many prohibitionists. Here too, such UAVs cannot be considered "autonomous" machines.[12] Just like commercial planes, UAVs are equipped with auto-pilot that is able to manage the machine under certain conditions; the auto-pilot is using the mechanical and electronic systems to follow a flight plan, stabilize speed and height ... But, when it comes to the lethal functions of the Predator or the Reaper, the machine is no such thing as an "auto-firing" program; the killing function is remotely controlled by a dedicated military unit.[13] The missile if fired by a human operator along with legal rules of engagement, under the control and responsibility of a chain of command which may include the US President himself. Accordingly, a Predator drone is not closer to an autonomous system than an Airbus or a Boeing plane can be.

Another weapons systems which could fit with the concept of LAWS, are the Israeli Iron Dome, the South-Korean SGAR-A1 or the US Phalanx CIWS anti-missile defense system. The latter is a gun-based close-in weapon system designed to defend military watercraft automatically against incoming threats such as aircraft, missiles, small boats ... Once activated, the Phalanx system can automatically search for, detect, track, engage, and confirm kills using its computer-controlled radar system. However, the Phalanx is not considered as problematic by NGOs such as the Campaign to Stop Killer Robots for at least three interesting reasons.[14] First, a human decision is required to authorize weapons release. Second, the system operates within tight parameters in relatively controlled environments. Third, it offers an opportunity for a human

12 Jean-François Caron, 'Defining Semi-Autonomous, Automated and Autonomous Weapon Systems in Order to Understand Their Ethical Challenges' (2020) 1 Digital War 173.

13 Thomas B Lukaszewicz, 'Joint Doctrine and UAV Employment.' (NAVAL WAR COLL NEWPORT RI 1996); Sarah Kerrigan, 'PREVENTING CIVILIAN CASUALTIES: ACCOUNTABILITY AND OVERSIGHT FOR DRONE CONTRACTORS' (2020) 49 Public Contract Law Journal 735.

14 Bode and Watts (n 9).

override. The combination of the three criteria is of particular interest. From this combination may be inferred two different approaches to "human control". The first one is a "direct control mode" on what the machine is doing; this control may be on site (Phalanx ICWS) or remotely located (Predator or Reaper) The human operator is supposed to be able to abort the system in case of a wrong decision. The second one is an "indirect control mode" which may rely on a human decision to release the system and preprogrammed tight rules of functioning. In the case of the Phalanx CIWS system, these rules include multiple criteria to identify a threat and engage it: the range of the target increasing or decreasing in relation to the ship, the capability of the target to maneuver and hit the ship, the range of velocity in which the target is moving … Weapons systems such as Iron Dome, SGAR-A1 or Phalanx could be labeled "automated" systems, which means that they are not "fully autonomous systems". The machine is under human supervision since its decisions are exhaustively determined by parameters and algorithms chosen by human beings.

Once these weapons systems defined and labelled as "non autonomous", two different approaches remain as far as the definition of "autonomy" is at stake. For Philosophers, "autonomy" is the privilege of an agent who is "first and foremost able to pose a deliberate and independent action that results from his own will".[15] The deliberative process the agent is implementing takes into account the difference between right and wrong, includes and weighs different moral principles and values, does not abide by preprogrammed rules which deprive him from his own arbitration. Technically, building an "autonomous machine" would require strong artificial intelligence which will not exist in a near future.

For numerous engineers, this philosophical approach to "autonomy" is misleading since "autonomy" or "intelligence" are strictly human characteristics and cannot be used to define the functioning of a machine.[16] For the French "Defense Ethics Committee", an autonomous weapons system does not define its own rules.[17] "Behind autonomy, there are automatisms; behind the automatisms, there are programs; behind the programs, there are humans who set

---

15 Caron (n 12).

16 Catherine Tessier, 'Autonomie': Polysémie, Confusion, Éthique' [2022] Le Magazine des ingénieurs de l'armement 68.

17 Comité d'éthique de la Défense, 'Avis Sur l'intégration de l'autonomie Des Systèmes d'armes Létaux.' (*MInistère des Armées*, 29 April 2021) <https://www.defense.gouv.fr/salle-de-presse/communiques/communique_le-comite-d-ethique-de-la-defense-publie-son-rapport-sur-l-integration-de-l-autonomie-des-systemes-d-armes-letaux> accessed 6 November 2021; Didier Danet, 'Pourquoi La France a Renoncé Aux SALA' [2022] DSI (Défense et Sécurité Internationale) 98.

the rules of the machine, including those authorizing this machine to be freed from these same rules." Therefore, the Committee establishes a clear distinction between two categories of lethal weapons systems.[18]

Fully autonomous lethal weapon systems "are programmed to be able to go beyond the initial employment framework and change their operating rules to make a decision for an action without situation assessment by the chain of command." In regard to this definition, an autonomous system is not a free agent who makes his own decision according to a set of legal and moral considerations; it is a computerized machine which can overpass the program defined by the military chain of command and undertakes a new mission that involves possible life and death decisions.

LAWS are thus distinguished from weapon systems based on automation[19] that "are lethal weapon systems whose decision functions (in the sense of robotic decision-making autonomy) are dependent on a specific action framework (SALIA). SALIA cannot take lethal initiatives that would lead it to modify its field of operation." After assessing the situation and under its responsibility, the military in charge can assign, in a limited space-time and under certain conditions, the execution of tasks in certain critical functions, such as identification, classification, interception, engagement of specific targets. This reminds us of the criterium based on the release of the weapons system. SALIAs must include technical guarantees or intrinsic features preventing flaws, misappropriation and renunciation by the chain of command of two essential prerogatives, namely situation assessment and reporting.

The two visions of autonomy are very different one from the other. Autonomy in the philosophical meaning comes to the conclusion that no "autonomous machine" will ever exist since "free will" is specific to the human species, strong artificial intelligence being a myth for science fiction novelists. The technical definition assumes that autonomous systems may exist, based on computer programs deliberately designed to authorize the machine to change the assigned mission and decide of life and death according to undefined algorithms. The committee immediately states that such "autonomous" systems would be unacceptable for many reasons. They would not comply with legal requirements of Humanitarian Law such as proportionality or discrimination. They also would infringe fundamental principles of military Ethics: honor, dignity, controlled use of force, humanity.

18 Non lethal weapons systems (such as "assistants" are put apart by the Committee).

19 In French, the relevant acronym to designate such non autonomous systems is SALIA).

Beyond differences between philosophers and engineers, both recommend that military application of scientific innovations should not lead to the development of LAWS. Following this conclusion, major industrial countries such as the UK or France have publicly stated that they will not develop nor use LAWS on the battlefield. The question is then: how to explain that these countries do not support a ban on LAWS if they do not intend to develop them? Why do they refuse an international agreement which would prohibit the kind of weapons they publicly disapprove? Do hypocrisy and cynicism prevail in conducting international relations? One may think so. But it may be demonstrated that ethical aims must fit with technical constraints inherent to the law building process and that this is not the case as far as LAWS prohibition is at stake.

2.2 *"Killer Robots": Why the Failure of Negotiations Is Not So Big Deal*

In spite of long and repeated sessions in Geneva, no shared definition of "Autonomous Systems" emerged and the discord is so intense that no consensus is to be reached in a near future. Therefore, no explicit prohibition of LAWS should occur very soon. Does this mean that autonomous weapons systems will be developed and implemented without any restriction? Is there some kind of legal void or "black hole" in which weapons producers and the military will rush in without any consideration for ethical issues?

In our opinion, there is no such thing as a "legal void" in the case of "autonomous weapons systems".[20] These systems fall under the general rules of additional protocols to Geneva Convention. There is no doubt that the legal provisions of the First Additional Protocol to the Geneva Conventions (esp. Article 36) are relevant and that autonomous weapons systems must comply with its requirements. Article 36 states that 'in the study, development, acquisition or adoption of any new weapon, means or method of warfare, a High Contracting Party is under an obligation to determine whether its use would be prohibited, in any or all circumstances, by the provisions of this Protocol or by any other rule of international law applicable to that High Contracting Party.'[21] Like any innovation in military equipment, autonomous lethal weapons systems fall within the scope of the general framework of Article 36. Any

20 Didier Danet, 'Un Enfer Pavé de Bonnes Intentions: Interdire Les Killer Robots', *Drones et killer robots: Faut-il les interdire?* (Presses Universitaires de Rennes 2015).

21 Isabelle Daoust, Robin Coupland and Rikke Ishoey, 'New Wars, New Weapons? The Obligation of States to Assess the Legality of Means and Methods of Warfare' (2002) 84 International Review of the Red Cross 345; Natalia Jevglevskaja, 'States' Weapons Review Obligations under Article 36 of the 1977 Additional Protocol I to the Geneva Conventions and beyond' (PhD Thesis, University of Melbourne 2018).

country developing such systems would therefore be obliged to ensure that they comply with the rules of international humanitarian law, first and foremost the principles of discrimination or proportionality.[22] If we consider that LAWS would not be able to comply with Humanitarian Law requirements, which are in line with fundamental ethical principles, an effective prohibition already exists in the positive current legislation.

We do not intend to discuss in this paper the content and modalities of application of Article 36. Our point is to insist on the fact that, in the absence of an explicit prohibition of LAWS due to the failure of Geneva negotiations, the general regime of Article 36 prohibits every military innovation that could not be proven consistent with the provisions of law.

It could be argued that particular conventions already prohibit certain weapons: blinding lasers, ammunition containing non-detectable fragments, etc.[23] A common feature of these special agreements is that they deal with well-defined objects and that most stakeholders agree on the unethical dimension of these weapons. No debate hampers the agenda for years without resulting in a consensual definition of what is at stake. Defining a blinding laser and the features of such an equipment does not give rise to endless controversies. The same for non-detectable fragments of ammunition. This is not the case for LAWS, for which there is currently no agreement to define and characterize them.

A ban on 'autonomous weapons systems' would therefore raise continuing difficulties in defining the nature and characteristics of new weapons systems that increasingly incorporate automated functions but are not fully autonomous. Endless conflicts would develop as to which regime should apply to which innovation: specific prohibition or the general regime of Article 36. Instead of strengthening the desired control, a specific regime would only weaken it and plunge it into endless questions of interpretation.

To conclude this first part of the paper, we consider that the failure of negotiations in order to ban LAWS which took place in Geneva, does not mean that military innovations can spread without any sort of legal or ethical constraints.

---

22 Chengeta (n 7).

23 Burrus M Carnahan and Marjorie Robertson, 'The Protocol on' Blinding Laser Weapons': A New Direction for International Humanitarian Law.' (1996) 90 The American Journal of International Law 90.3 (1996): 484–490. 484; Bengt Anderberg, Ove E Bring and Myron L Wolbarsht, 'Blinding Laser Weapons and International Humanitarian Law' (1992) 29 Journal of Peace Research 287; Louise Doswald-Beck, 'New Protocol on Blinding Laser Weapons' (1996) 36 International Review of the Red Cross (1961–1997) 272; Ann Peters, 'Blinding Laser Weapons: New Limits on the Technology of Warfare' (1995) 18 Loy. LA Int'l & Comp. LJ 733.

Arms producers and military forces are not free to create and implement weapons that would not be able to comply with legal provisions of the International Humanitarian Law. Autonomous systems as well as automated or remote control systems must be compliant with legal and ethical principles such as the discrimination or the proportionality principles. The terrifying Terminator, whatever its real autonomy, does not and it would be prohibited under the general provisions of Article 36. No additional gap between Law and Ethics is rising due to the specific issue of growing automation of modern weapons.

3 Law, Ethics and Military Innovation

The case of LAWS is a good starting point to explore the issues related to military spillovers of innovations which occur in the most important fields of the fourth industrial revolution: computers sciences, telecommunications, energy, biology … These scientific discoveries raise societal concerns and ethical questions which go on increasing when the military bring into play.[24] Are existing set of legal rules able to fit with new applications of science? Are ethical concerns efficiently taken into account? Is the Law an effective ground to promote societal concerns and enforce ethical principles?

According to the famous legal academic Mireille Delmas-Marty, the existing provisions of the Law may be used through legal strategies to protect and promote ethical principles in three different ways.[25]

3.1 *Resisting Dehumanization without Creating New Legal Rules*

First, existing provisions in domestic and international law provide a strong basis for regulating or resisting certain dehumanizing effects of scientific and technological progress, whether in civil areas such as medicine, security or in military applications such as weapons systems. There is no need for new legal norms each time a new weapons system is developed and manufactured.

---

24 Amitai Etzioni, 'Pros and Cons of Autonomous Weapons Systems (with Oren Etzioni)', *Happiness is the wrong metric* (Springer 2018); Max van Kralingen, 'Use of Weapons: Should We Ban the Development of Autonomous Weapons Systems?' (2016) 18 The International Journal of Intelligence, Security, and Public Affairs 132; Steven Umbrello, Phil Torres and Angelo F De Bellis, 'The Future of War: Could Lethal Autonomous Weapons Make Conflict More Ethical?' (2020) 35 AI & SOCIETY 273.

25 Mireille Delmas-Marty, *Une Boussole Des Possibles. Gouvernance Mondiale et Humanismes Juridiques: Leçon de Clôture Prononcée Le 11 Mai 2011* (Collège de France 2020); Mireille Delmas-Marty and Marie-Françoise Chevallier-Le Guyader, 'Le Principe de Précaution: Équilibrer Innovation et Conservation' [2018] Raison presente 69.

General principles are broadly applicable to new circumstances where there is a willingness to interpret them in the light of those circumstances. Napoleon did not know about e-mail, yet the secrecy of correspondence established in the Civil Code applies without difficulty to handwritten letters sent by post as well as to e-mails sent by electronic means.[26] In the case of LAWS, Article 36 provides a legal framework that is perfectly suited to regulate military innovations of all kinds. New weapons systems would not be better regulated because a new legal standard would have been enacted in the wake of their emergence. Based on this very simple idea, the French Defence Ethics Committee defined a set of conditions in order to assess military innovations based on automated functioning. In particular, it requires that five cumulative conditions be met for the increasing automation of weapons systems to be acceptable.

1) The system must be integrated into a chain of command that is free from loopholes or missing links. 2) It must not have any possibility of being reprogrammed by itself. 3) It must correspond in all respects to the properties stipulated by the Ministry of Defence. 4) It must be transparent to the commissioner. 5) It must be socially acceptable. It is therefore possible to regulate the development of technical and scientific progress on the basis of existing law, interpreted in the light of ethical considerations specific to French values and principles without waiting for a hypothetical ban to be enacted in the form of a dedicated international agreement. It is also inferred that doing nothing while waiting for the adoption of a useless legal norm that will probably never occur is an unacceptable position from a moral point of view.

3.2 *Making Global Stakeholders Accountable*

According to Mireille Delmas-Marty, making clear that military innovation falls under the rule of existing laws enforces the accountability of global actors in political institutions, research centers, industry and armed forces. Since the 1990s, the personal responsibility of political and military leaders has been under greater scrutiny. Some of them have been targeted by international courts, in particular to hold them accountable for the war crimes they inspired

26 Brahim ATROUCH, 'La Protection Des Données Personnelles Du Salarié' (2021) 1 Journal of Integrated Studies In Economics, Law, Technical Sciences & Communication; Marc Richevaux, 'Nouvelles Technologies de l'information et de La Communication Vie Privée Des Salariés et Responsabilité Pénale' (2001); Martine Bourrie-Quenillet and Florence Rodhain, 'L'utilisation de La Messagerie Électronique Dans l'entreprise. Aspects Juridiques et Managériaux En France et Aux Etats-Unis.' [2002] La Semaine juridique-édition générale 63; Yohei Suda, 'La Surveillance Des E-Mails et La Protection Des Données Des Employés Dans Le Secteur Privé: Les Comparaisons Du Présent et Du Futur Entre l'Europe de l'Ouest et Les États-Unis' (2003) 16 Revue juridique de l'Ouest 461.

or committed.[27] The growing degree of automation in military weapons systems may have similar consequences for researchers who design the systems and manufacturers who build them. Let's suppose that during a military campaign, the implementation of an automated weapons system causes civilian casualties due to an error in the targets selection process. The military chain of command will be under scrutiny and the accountability of the officer in charge will be questioned. But, the potential responsibility of those who conceived and manufactured the system will be under scrutiny as well.[28] Involving not only the people who implement a machine but also those who conceived it is nothing but new. It is a well established principle in civil liability case law. Since the XIXth century, judges differentiate custody of the structure and custody of the behavior if a machine failing is involved in an accident. The user's accountability takes precedence in the later while the manufacturer is responsible if the conception or the making of the machine is the reason why it failed.[29] The greater the degree of autonomy granted to the weapons system, the more the guardianship of the structure will be questioned, with the result that the actors in research and industry will be called into question. Academics, engineers or executives may have to face prosecutions in the decades to come.

This new balance of responsibilities between civilian designers and military users seems to us to be fair and even desirable. It will force scientists and engineers to leave their comfortable position of signing petitions condemning

27 John Hagan, 'Justice in the Balkans', *Justice in the Balkans* (University of Chicago Press 2010); Victor Peskin, *International Justice in Rwanda and the Balkans: Virtual Trials and the Struggle for State Cooperation* (Cambridge University Press 2008); Aleksandar R Ivanović and Lars Petter Soltvedt, 'Investigating and Prosecuting War Crimes in the Western Balkans.' (2016) 18 Varstvoslovje: Journal of Criminal Justice & Security; Jelena Obradovic, *Ethnic Conflict and War Crimes in the Balkans: The Narratives of Denial in Post-Conflict Serbia* (Bloomsbury Publishing 2013).

28 Thompson Chengeta, 'Accountability Gap: Autonomous Weapon Systems and Modes of Responsibility in International Law' (2016) 45 Denv. J. Int'l L. & Pol'y 1; Daniel N Hammond, 'Autonomous Weapons and the Problem of State Accountability' (2014) 15 Chi. J. Int'l L. 652; Tetyana Krupiy, 'Regulating a Game Changer: Using a Distributed Approach to Develop an Accountability Framework for Lethal Autonomous Weapon Systems' (2018) 50 Geo. J. Int'l L. 45; Diego Mauri, 'Autonomous Weapons Systems and the Accountability Gap Conundrum', *Autonomous Weapons Systems and the Protection of the Human Person* (Edward Elgar Publishing 2022); Elliot Winter, 'The Accountability of Software Developers for War Crimes Involving Autonomous Weapons: The Role of the Joint Criminal Enterprise Doctrine' (2021) 83 U. Pitt. L. Rev. 51.

29 Kamil Antaki, 'Garde De Structure Et Garde De Comportement' (1966) 12 McGill LJ 41; Jean-Pierre Sutto, 'Garde de La Structure et Garde Du Comportement' (1965) 15 RJT os 72; Thérèse Rousseau-Houle, 'Les Lendemains de l'arrêt Kravitz: La Responsabilité Du Fabricant Dans Une Perspective de Réforme' (1980) 21 Les Cahiers de droit 5.

the use of their work for military purposes[30] without considering the fact that this work is ambivalent and that, as Mireille Delmas-Marty states it, isolating military applications from civilian applications in order to prohibit the former is not an option anymore. Military and civilian applications are the two inseparable sides of a unique coin. The question that academics and engineers must face is the following: considering that a scientific discovery will have both civilian and military applications, should ethical concerns lead them to reject or reframe the discovery itself?

3.3 *Balancing Precaution and Action*

According to Mireille Delmas-Marty, society expects the law to provide a process for balancing the precautionary principle and the need to act.[31] In the Western world in general, the precautionary principle has gained a lot of ground in recent times. In France, for example, it has been incorporated into the Constitution and now stands in the highest layers of legal standards.[32] The precautionary principle has been widely used to stop the development of major infrastructures in many areas of activity, including transport or trade.[33] But an abusive interpretation of the precautionary principle leads to the paralysis of any significant infrastructure. It is therefore a potential threat for research and innovation which, by their very nature, change the world. A primary goal for the legislator and the judges is to keep an acceptable balance between the desire to preserve the world as it exists today and the aim to change it for a better one. As far as weapons systems are at stake, the gap between the respective positions of the different stakeholders or the seriousness of political, human or ethical stakes makes it difficult to establish the relevant and consensual balance. No single legal rule is rich enough to embrace all the cases. A step-by-step approach, combining different types of rules is required. In the case of LAWS, the Geneva failure demonstrates that an international convention agreed by

30 Forrest E Morgan and others, 'Military Applications of Artificial Intelligence: Ethical Concerns in an Uncertain World' (RAND PROJECT AIR FORCE SANTA MONICA CA SANTA MONICA United States 2020); Scott Shane and Daisuke Wakabayashi, '"The Business of War": Google Employees Protest Work for the Pentagon' (2018) 4 The New York Times.

31 Delmas-Marty and Chevallier-Le Guyader (n 25).

32 Laurence Baghestani-Perrey, 'La Valeur Juridique Du Principe de Précaution' (2000) 25 Revue juridique de l'Environnement 19; Julien Bétaille, 'Le Principe de Précaution, Un 'droit' Garanti Par La Constitution?' (2016) 105 Revue francaise de droit constitutionnel e29; Sylvie Caudal, 'Les Impacts de La Constitutionnalisation Du Principe de Précaution En Droit de l'urbanisme' (2020) 62 Archives de philosophie du droit 323.

33 Gérald Bronner and Etienne Géhin, *L'inquiétant Principe de Précaution* (Presses universitaires de France 2010); Caudal (n 32); Jean-Marie Legay, 'Sur Le Principe de Précaution'.

all countries involved in the negotiation is not the relevant approach. But, the absence of this international agreement does not mean that LAWS can spread in a legal black hole. Many binding rules regulate automated weapons from the conception to the implementation on the battlefield. The central set of legal provisions is lying in the general principles of the International Humanitarian Law. Besides this core set of rules, stakeholders may develop other kinds of rules: voluntarily constraining engagements, codes of conduct, national scrutiny procedures.

What must be remembered is that in a complex world where innovation is often more ambivalent than ambiguous, the balance between precaution and action can certainly not be included in a single text adopted once and for all. This balance requires progressive adjustments and multiple commitments, with the law or international convention being only one modality among others. Going down the road of a major international text signed by States with contradictory interests is the best way to achieve nothing. It would undoubtedly be more useful to envisage more contractual forms of regulation with the different stakeholders.

4 Conclusion

The failure of the NGO campaign for an international convention banning lethal autonomous weapons systems demonstrates the limits of legal strategies developed over the past decades to defend societal causes. These legal strategies (lobbying and litigation) were seen as a powerful lever for change.[34] They have been widely used to promote important causes, such as the environment or human rights. However, these campaigns need to balance the logic and principles of political rhetoric with the specific characteristics of legal techniques. This is why the 'campaign to stop Killer Robots' was destined to fail from the point of view of normative production. The term 'Killer Robot' is certainly a very good buzzword for communication purposes. However, banning

34 Pieter Bouwen and Margaret McCown, 'Lobbying versus Litigation: Political and Legal Strategies of Interest Representation in the European Union' (2007) 14 Journal of European Public Policy 422; John M De Figueiredo and Rui JP De Figueiredo, 'The Allocation of Resources by Interest Groups: Lobbying, Litigation and Administrative Regulation' (2002) 4 Business and Politics 161; Paul H Rubin, Christopher Curran and John F Curran, 'Litigation versus Legislation: Forum Shopping by Rent Seekers' (2001) 107 Public Choice 295; Claude Champaud and Didier Danet, *Stratégies Judiciaires Des Entreprises* (Dalloz-Sirey 2006).

something that does not exist, that cannot be defined or characterized correctly and that is already regulated by long-established texts does not meet the conditions required for the emergence of an international legal standard.

Does this mean that the law is a 'paper tiger' that is useless when it comes to regulating the innovation processes of the large digital companies, especially in the military domain? Does this mean that the law is powerless to deal with the wave of change of the fourth industrial revolution?

Following Mireille Delmas-Marty, we consider that the Law can serve three objectives when it comes to designing and implementing a process for regulating major innovations:

Existing laws often contain the necessary basis to resist the dehumanising drifts of technical, political, economic transformations ... Not every new challenge requires new legal provisions. It is essential to get rid of the idea that the Law has to be rewritten every time an innovation appears. The primary characteristic of a well-made law is its generality and its capacity to be applied independently of the circumstances of the moment, of which the degree of technical evolution is one of the many components. The absence of a text explicitly mentioning such and such a technical innovation should not therefore lead to the conclusion that it is not subject to any regulation and that anyone can do anything. The net of legal norms is sufficiently wide and tight for very few technical innovations to develop in the 'legal vacuum'.

Existing laws holds the global players of the fourth industrial revolution to account. In our view, the failure of the lobbying strategy at the CCCW should lead the promoters of the 'Campaign to Stop Killer Robots' to turn to a litigation strategy. On the basis of existing law, this litigation campaign would take the form of legal proceedings against companies suspected of developing weapons systems that incorporate automated processes that question an effective control of its behavior by the military user: specifications that do not respond to the command, non-transparent code that prohibits knowledge of the detailed functioning of the machine, databases that are insufficient to allow learning adapted to the complexity of the operational context, etc. The target of these high-profile lawsuits would then be less the military actors than the companies and research institutions. These lawsuits would have little chance of success, but they would serve, with the help of the media, as a 'sounding board' to re-launch the debate in public opinion. They would also force civil actors (companies, researchers, etc.) to take responsibility for the very principle of certain research. An interesting example has just been given by Microsoft, which recently announced that it would no longer develop and sell an emotion recognition tool, as this type of software has no established scientific validity.

It is not a question of refusing certain applications (security or military) of emotion recognition software but of not engaging in research at all.[35]

Existing laws aim at finding an acceptable balance between the precautionary principle and the need to act. No society can remain fixed in the sole conservation of what exists. It must adapt, change and progress. As Mireille Delmas-Marty points it out, innovation is ambivalent more than ambiguous. This means that the social acceptability of innovations must be considered as a whole, not being able to distinguish between good and bad applications. In this respect, the action of the 'Campaign to stop Killer Robots' bears witness to an outdated, obsolete approach that is unsuited to the nature of the fourth industrial revolution. This revolutionary process can only be legally and ethically regulated by a multi-faceted approach, based not on a single and sacred norm but on a variety of different norms ranging from self-regulation (e.g. company R&D policies) to international norms (e.g. Article 36), but also to best practice guides, professional standards or national laws. All these regulatory norms will necessarily merge in a heterogeneous, shifting, sometimes redundant or contradictory block. However, the extent of the transformations underway, as well as the importance of the ethical, economic and technical issues at stake, makes it impossible to believe that a single standard can provide definitive answers to each and every questions. Some may be sorry to hear this, but it seems certain that even the most stable societies have never functioned otherwise.

35 James Vincent, 'Microsoft to Retire Controversial Facial Recognition Tool That Claims to Identify Emotion' (*The Verge*, 21 June 2022) <https://www.theverge.com/2022/6/21/23177016/microsoft-retires-emotion-recognition-azure-ai-tool-api> accessed 13 July 2022; Elliott Lewis, 'Microsoft Is Removing Emotion Recognition Features from Its Facial Recognition Tech' (*NBC News*, 27 June 2022) <https://www.nbcnews.com/tech/tech-news/microsoft-removing-emotion-recognition-features-facial-recognition-tec-rcna35087> accessed 13 July 2022.

CHAPTER 3

New Technologies and the Enhanced Soldier: Ethical Approval and Ethical Boundaries for European Nations

Gérard de Boisboissel

1 Survey Overview

1.1 *Assumptions Made*

The augmentation techniques described in this survey assume that the following prerequisites are met by civil, medical and military authorities, prior to the use of any enhancement technologies:

1. Any augmentation technique that has an effect on humans requires their initial consent before it is implemented.
2. Any augmentation technique should meet a clearly defined operational need, validated in advance by the political authorities, and must obtain the agreement of the medical community.
3. Any augmentation technique is considered here only in the context of armed conflict.

1.2 *Objectives*

This study aims to provide elements of context on the perception of different enhancement techniques by professionals in the military community or among researchers interested in combatants and their physiological limits.

It intends to give an outline of the approval of potential enhancement techniques having an effect on the combatant's body, by indicating the sensitivities of each professional category (medical officers, soldiers, researchers) and of each European country, if any.

The ultimate purpose of this study is to initiate a debate among European ethicists and within the military community, which could be based on the data collected by the survey, and which could feed future reflection among EuroIsme members on the following subjects:

1. Is it acceptable to use technologies that have an effect on the soldier's body for better military efficiency?

 | DOI:10.1163/9789004544314_005

2. What boundaries should be set at European level, bearing in mind that other countries in the world potentially have a different ethical approach to that of Europe?
3. How can we limit the hybridisation of man and machine that enables the soldier to be integrated directly into a weapon system and to wage war at a distance with his brain alone?

1.3 *About This Survey*

Basically, this survey is meant to cover the entire possible spectrum of enhancement techniques. This can be summed up as follows:
- Non-invasive technologies allowing to acquire new skills,
- Invasive techniques on the human body: implants, pharmacology,
- Irreversible anthropotechnics (increased visual and auditory acuity, morphological changes).
- The survey has been conducted on behalf of the CReC Saint-Cyr in view of the Budapest 2022 EuroIsme conference.
- It was anonymous but the nationality of the person was requested,
- It was open to military personnel, the military medical community and to researchers working on defense issues,
- It was accessible via a web link hosted at the Saint-Cyr Military Academy,
- It was conducted among representatives of each nation, through the contacts of EuroIsme members from March to May 2022,
- The survey was closed just after the EuroIsme conference.

2 Methodological Choices

The questionnaire was first translated into three languages (English, French and German) to allow a better understanding of the specificity of the questions asked and to avoid any misunderstanding. It was then reviewed by several researchers. The term "enhancement" was chosen here instead of the term "augmentation" which is nevertheless beginning to appear in the scientific literature. The people polled in this survey were all approached directly by a member of Euro-ISME or by the Euro-ISME Newsletter. The survey was mainly carried out via a page on the website of the Saint-Cyr military academy, which ensured the cybersecurity of the data collected. Ten people were personally asked to participate during the Euro-ISME conference in Budapest, to fill out the questionnaire on paper, not nominally, and to give it back directly to the author of these lines.

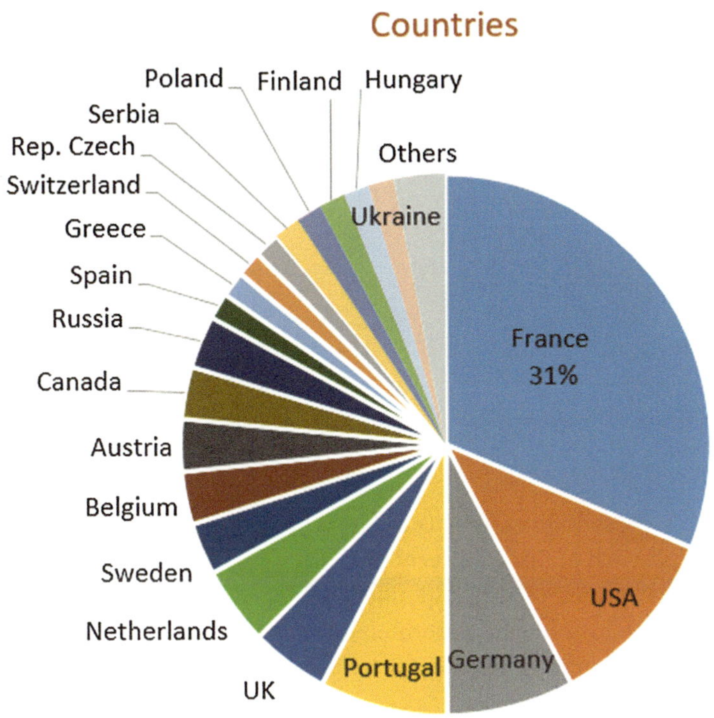

FIGURE 3.1 Countries of origin of respondents

For a good understanding of the results by the readers, a global approach was proposed, admittedly simplifying, but allowing an identical classification for the estimation of the minimum context where the use of an enhancement technique is justified, or for the type of military unit to which it can be implemented. In a similar way, the ethical impact was rated within a unique value scale. In the end, the graph models are thus simplified and identical for all the different enhancement techniques, allowing the reader to read and compare the results easily.

3 Overview of the 64 Participants

Sixty-four people participated. The author of this article is currently working in Saint-Cyr Coëtquidan, and thus had the opportunity to distribute this survey internally, which explains the high percentage of French responses. Nevertheless, European countries are overall quite well represented, even if it is difficult to be able to characterize the behavior of a specific country with

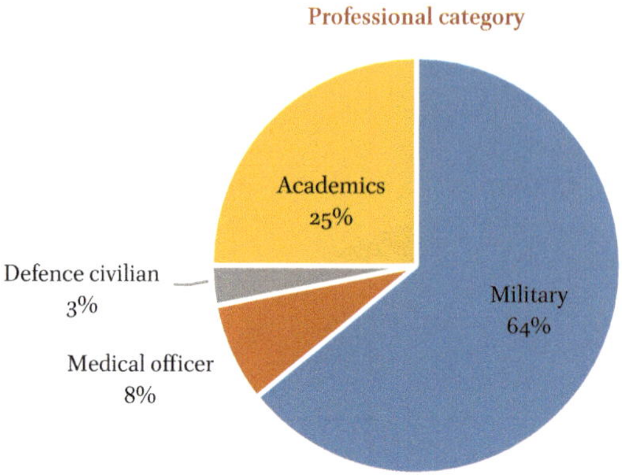

FIGURE 3.2 Professional occupation of respondents

only a few of its representatives. Twenty different countries represented makes the European approach of this study very credible.

Professional categories of the respondents show that two-thirds of the answers originate from soldiers, most often senior officers having command experience and, for some, experience in operational missions. Age categories are also distributed, which also gives credibility to the answers received. A quarter originates from academics, i.e., from university researchers who are members of the EuroIsme society and who work on ethical issues. 8% are medical officers.

Importantly, it should be noted that 4 of the 64 participants (6%) are totally against the very concept of enhancement. These are three French military as well as one European academic.

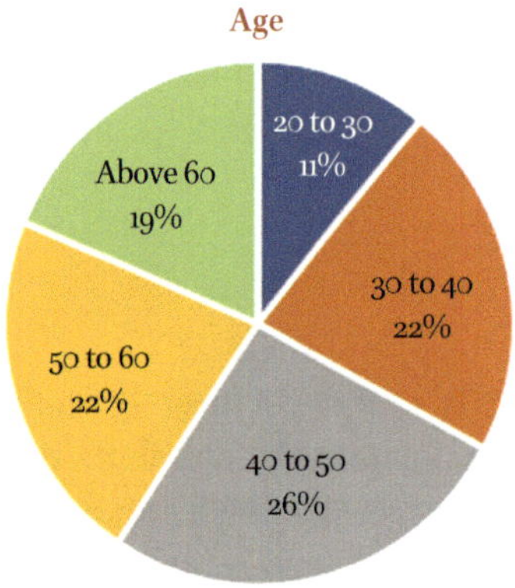

FIGURE 3.3 Age of respondents

This is indicative, in my opinion, of a certain distrust (or rejection) of enhancement by professionals who already have solid military experience.

Please note the answers of these 4 people totally against enhancement have been taken into account in all of the following graphs or percentage listed below.

4 Questions Asked

For each enhancement technique, the survey respondents were asked two questions:

1. If they think that the enhancement meets an operational need, and if so, the *minimum context where its use is justified*. The minimum context of use could be: a) Training (enhancement is possible as early as the training phase), b) Mission with controlled risk (a routine mission, not particularly risky), c) Risky mission, d) Extremely risky mission (danger is omnipresent in this mission), e) Survival (personal survival or fellow soldiers' survival is at stake), f) Or never.
   The minimal context obviously applies to the ensuing contexts. If a soldier can be enhanced for training, they can also be enhanced on missions with controlled risk, risky missions, etc.
   Please note: in certain cases where enhancement does not depend on the context but on the framework of use, the respondent was asked for *which type of military unit* the enhancement can be implemented: a) Conventional unit, b) Specialised unit (paratroopers, snipers), c) Special forces, d) None.
2. *The ethical impact*: give a rate on a scale of 1 to 10 (1 = no ethical impact, 10 = very high ethical stakes) concerning the ethical risks associated with the use of enhancement in the operational context you have chosen.

5 Results of the Survey

For each graph, the columns indicate the number of responses per category (left y axis), and the curve indicates the level of associated ethical risk (1 = no ethical impact, 10 = very high ethical stakes) (right y axis).[1]

---

1 Thanks to Lucile Chevallier for her help in building the graphs.

5.1 *Category: Technologies for Acquiring New Skills*

5.1.1 Equipment That Covers the Body

We consider here technologies carried by the combatant but without any invasive effect on the human body. We have in mind here exoskeletons or any other equipment accompanying the soldier in his mission and integrated into his/her equipment externally.

The question was: in what context do you think the use of equipment that constrains the body but provides real operational added value is justified? Examples: Exoskeletons, smart clothes.

For this type of enhancement, it seems that the majority of people think that enhancement equipment worn externally do not raise any particular ethical issues and we see a timid consensus on the use of these techniques for operational missions.

As a reminder, people opposed to any type of enhancement are included in this graph. We find them on the far-right side.

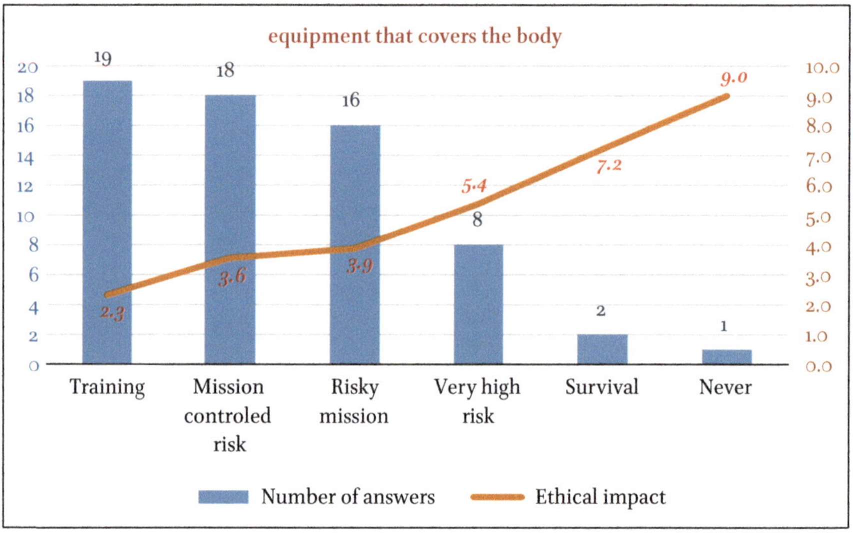

FIGURE 3.4 Context of use and ethical impact for the use of non-invasive equipment

5.1.2 Pre-processed Data Interfaces

Techniques proposed here are intelligent interfaces, possibly relying on Artificial Intelligence, that interface with the combatant's cognitive processes but in a non-invasive way: screens, glasses. These are, for example, decision support software or intelligent man/machine interfaces.

The question was: in what context do you think the use of interfaces can be justified if it enables the combatant to have access to a large amount of data, potentially pre-processed but constituting an additional mental burden? Examples: connected contact lenses, BCI*-type human-machine interfaces.*

We cannot see here many differences with the previous graph curve; the expected level of employment is identical. We nevertheless see a higher ethical concern, on average + 2 points.

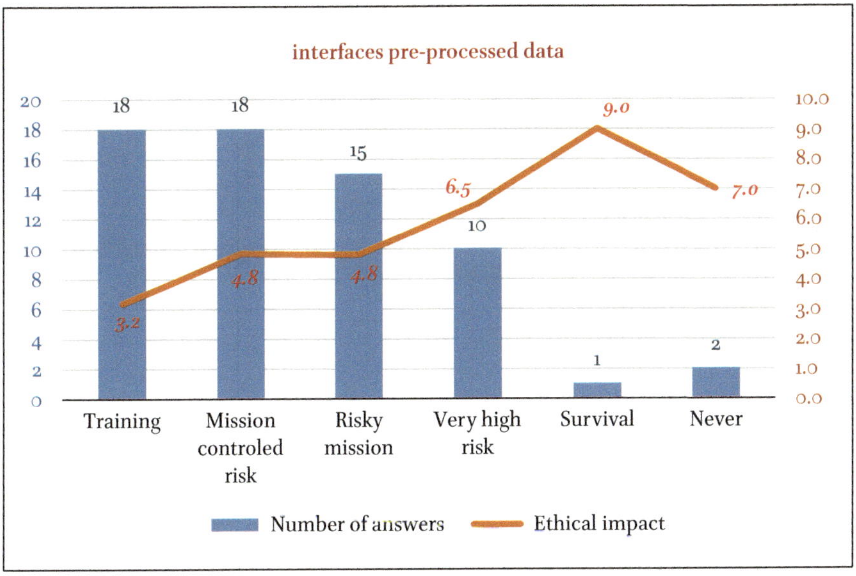

FIGURE 3.5 Context of use and ethical impact for interfacing with pre-processed data interfaces

5.1.3 Cognitive Stimuli

This enhancement process is different from the previous ones because, even if it is non-invasive, it involves effects on the human brain. The idea is to make the soldier react to stimuli, so that they can ultimately train their brain to react favorably to a particular situation: a kind of cerebral drill.

The question was: in what context do you think the use of techniques that develop the cognitive abilities of the combatant is justified? Examples: Neurofeedback stimulation that improves brain plasticity.

The reversible effect of these stimuli gives a fairly high approval rate of the technique. Few people are against it, but a majority envision its use only for military specialists.

Soldiers and medical officers consider that it can be used in specialized units, while academics think that it is better to use it only in Special Forces.

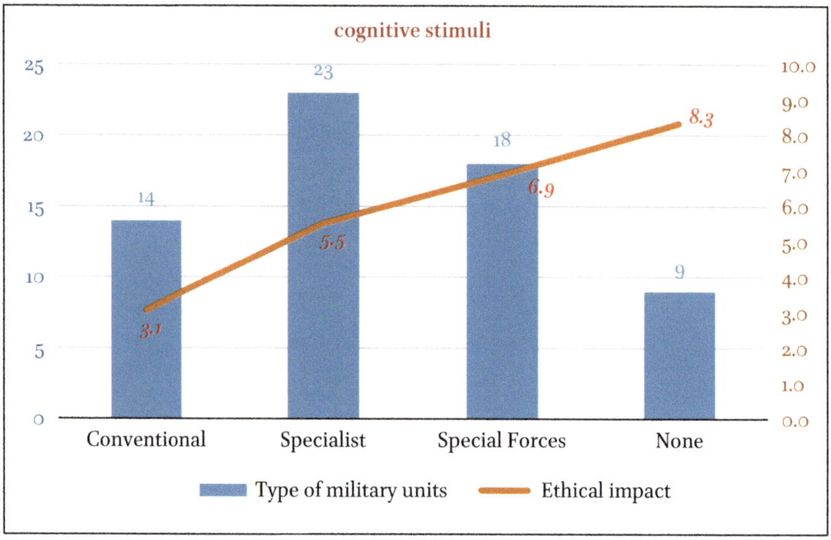

FIGURE 3.6 Ethical impact for developing cognitive abilities with stimuli and for which type of military unit

5.2 *Category: Pharmacology*

We are considering here invasive processes that have a direct effect on the human body, but are reversible.

Known since the dawn of humanity, the use of doping products or stimulating products for the human body and mind is not new for soldiers, but its use is nowadays extremely restricted or even nonexistent, due to the side effects that these substances may cause.

5.2.1 Substances That Trick the Body

The first category includes substances that will give false signals to the body, in order to deceive it. In particular, substances that suppress appetite or that reduce pain, or prevent you to sleep.

The question was: in what context do you think that taking substances to trick the body is justified? Examples: appetite suppressants, sleep aids, analgesics.

We see here a homogeneously different perception, which is relatively well distributed. This indicates a contrasting approach on the part of the respondents with 18% considering it always possible, the majority saying it should be restricted to risky cases. No general rejection, however (except for the 6% mentioned at the beginning of this paper).

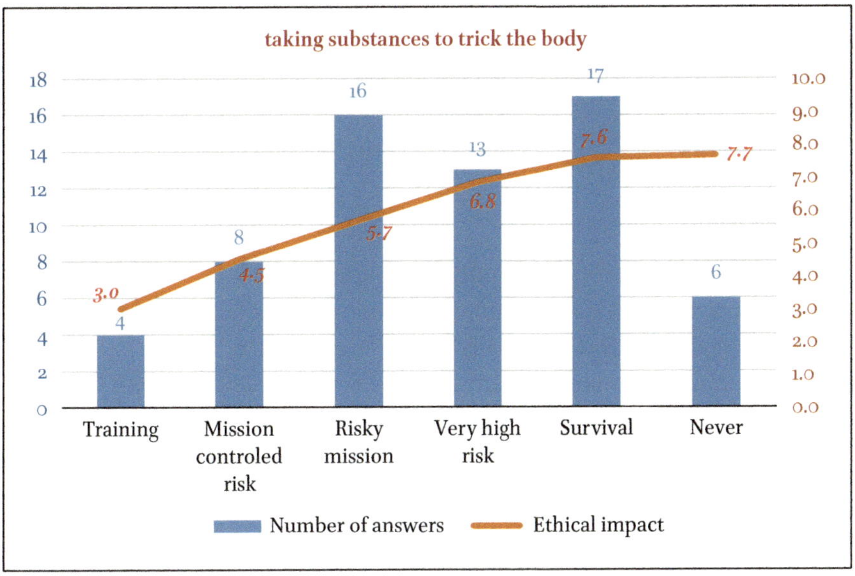

FIGURE 3.7 Context of use and ethical impact for taking substances that trick the body

5.2.2 Doping Substances

Here we deal with the case of very common uses in sports environment. Many soldiers may be tempted to copy such practices, especially if they consider they improve their combat performance for military effectiveness rather than for personal gain.

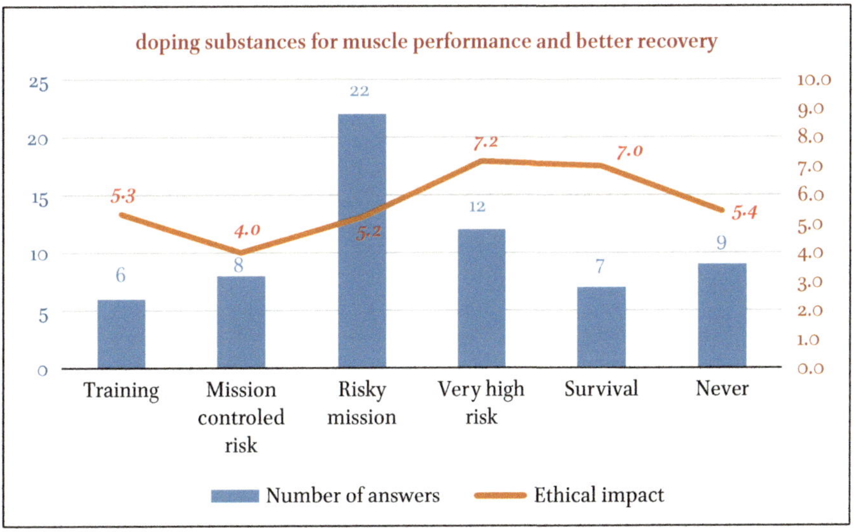

FIGURE 3.8 Context of use and ethical impact for doping substances

The question was: in what context do you think that taking doping substances for muscle performance and better recovery is justified?

We find here an influence of the practices of civil society on current practices in certain military units. The ethical impact is almost identical to that of the curve below, while alterations to the human body are significant. No noticeable rejection.

5.2.3 Boost Memory or Cognitive Attention

The use of psycho stimulants to boost cognitive attention is also a current practice in the civilian world, especially when people have to reach a certain level of intellectual performance (exams, complex and sustained work). If in civilian life these practices are assimilated to cheating, it may be different when the soldier is under threat or if a perfect execution of their mission is required to reduce the danger for others.

The question was: in what context do you think that taking substances to boost memory or cognitive abilities and attention is justified?

For 25% of the people, this use is acceptable whatever the context. More generally, there is an approval of this type of enhancement in the case of risky or very risky missions.

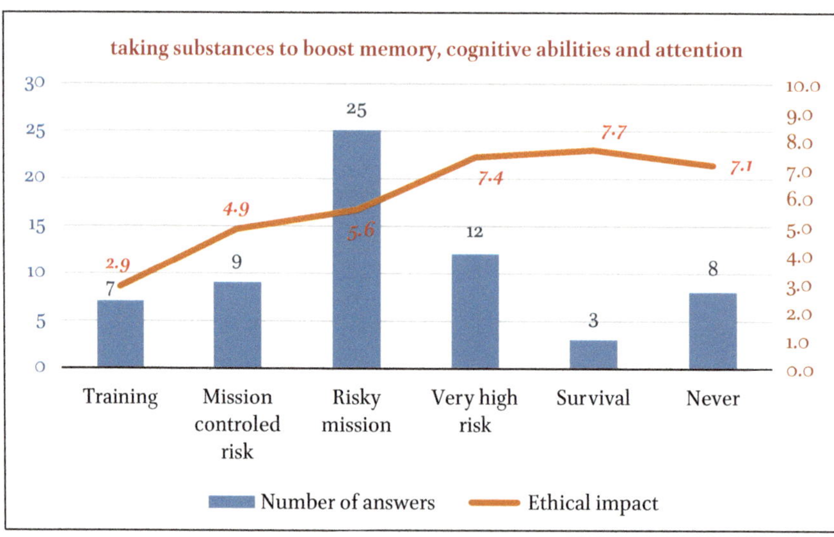

FIGURE 3.9 Context of use and ethical impact for taking substances to boost memory or cognitive attention

5.3 *Category: Implants*

We are now considering technological processes directly integrated into the human body, and thus purely invasive:

Firstly, to interface directly with an external system via a simple touch contact or via a wireless link, i.e., a remote personalized interface activated only by the chip. Just like currently in some Swedish companies, we can imagine soldiers working in very secure places being asked to equip themselves with a cyber-protected biometric chip, embedded under their skin, in order to ensure a better secured access to the building and to lock/unlock their workstations.

Secondly, to implant microchips subcutaneously in order to measure physiological data and, according to the measurement taken by the sensors, potentially release certain substances to enable the body to perform more efficiently.

We clearly see that the rejection rate is getting significant here and that ethical concern begins to be noticeable.

5.3.1 Intrabody Microchips

We consider here subcutaneous microchips that have no effect on the human body. They are just hosted by it. Applications could be automatic transmission of geolocation data, automatic transmission of monitoring data, etc.

The question was: in what context do you think that intrabody microchipping is justified? Examples: chips for geolocation, for access to ultra-secure sites or for physiological performance monitoring

If a big third of survey respondents approve, another third are against, and the remaining third approve if missions have a high level of risk.

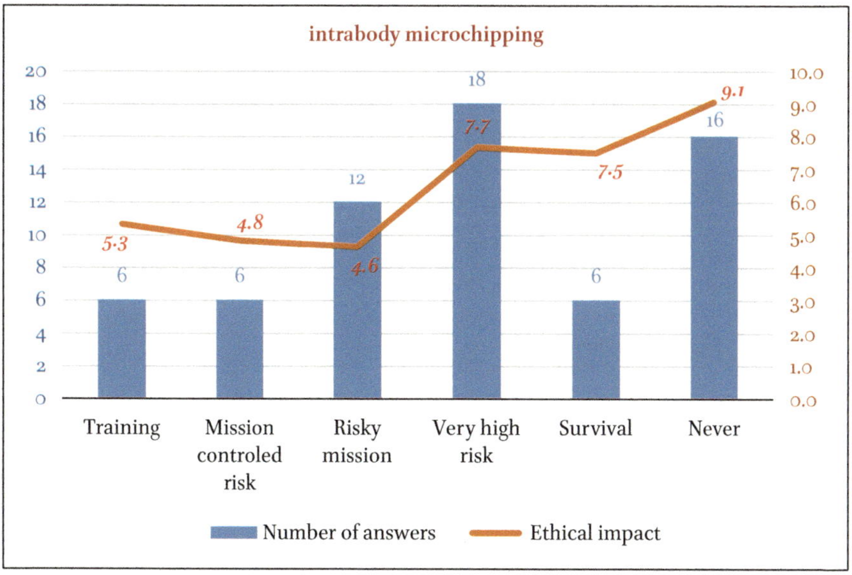

FIGURE 3.10 Context of use and ethical impact for using intrabody microchipping

5.3.2 Implants to Enhance Sensory and Physical Abilities

The implant can be used to boost human capacities (and not only repair deficiencies), or by making it possible to preserve these capacities over time.

It can be intelligent and analyze a concentration of toxins or hormones in blood, and automatically decide to release a substance that will enable the combatant to last longer in action, or reduce the risks of discomfort.

It can be an implant placed directly in contact with a muscle or organ, in order to stimulate it.

The question was: in what context do you think that the use of implants to enhance sensory and physical abilities is justified? Examples: retinal implants, muscle implants, micro-robots delivering medical substances according to physiological data

In more or less the same way as above, implants should be rejected according to one third of the people, with a very high ethical risk (almost the maximum). For another third, they can be considered only in extreme missions, or in specific working conditions.

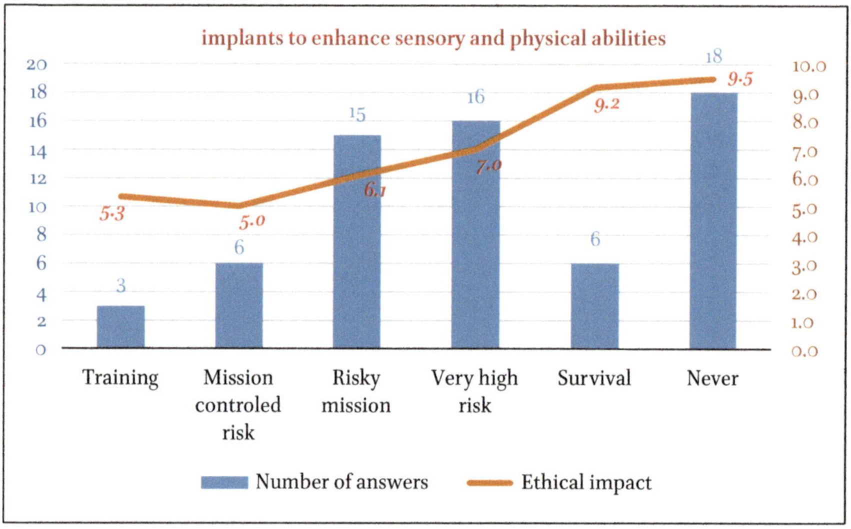

FIGURE 3.11 Context of use and ethical impact for using implants to enhance sensory and physical abilities

5.3.3 Hybridisation

A hybrid body is a body subjected to alteration for the purpose of enhancement or for a remote interaction with an external system. It is an artificial "crossbreeding" between Man and NBIC technologies.

The placement of subcutaneous implants will be seen here as hybridization because it will enable the human body to interact with the external remote activation of a system, etc.

Here we are faced with a major technological gap, with a door open on human beings fully integrated into an active military system that would be inoperative without them.

The question was: in what context do you think the implementation of human/machine hybridisation ensuring interconnection between the human body and external systems is justified? Examples: subcutaneous interfaces interconnected with external weapon systems

This graph is interesting because it shows a certain fear of the respondents about what hybridization is. Here we clearly face one of the major recommendations when enhancing the soldier: keep him in the loop of the weapon systems.

However, we note that only one eighth of the respondents approve of this notion and 44% reject it, or approve of it only in survival cases. It thus appears that this notion should be the topic of further research work in order to better

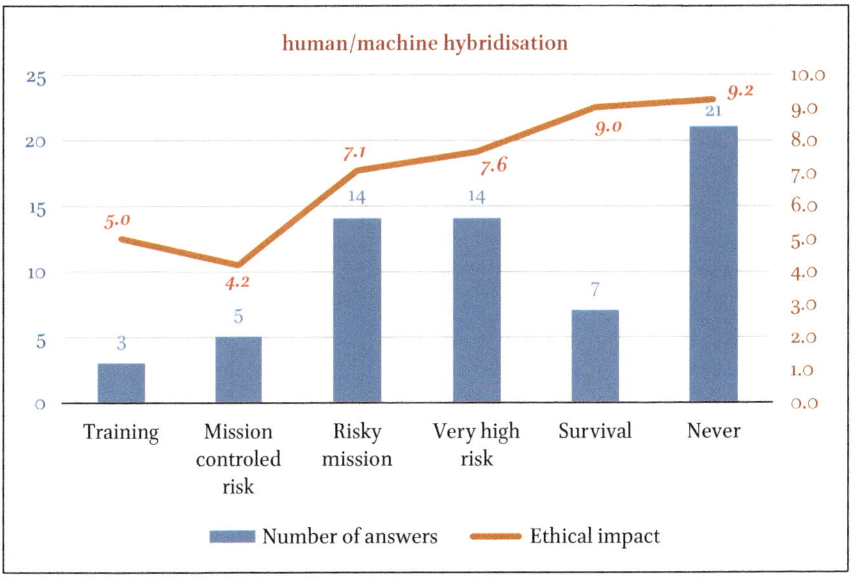

FIGURE 3.12 Context of use and ethical impact for human/machine hybridization

define what is meant by hybridisation and its impacts on soldiers but also on the systems managed by a soldier hybridized with these systems.

5.4 *Category: Anthropotechnics*

"Anthropotechnics is a modification that improves individual human performance, through an intervention on the human body, without medical purpose" (General Medical Officer Lionel Bourdon, 2015).

Here we consider the enhancement techniques that have direct effects on the human body but are irreversible, therefore at the heart of human ethical issues, but which are used in the military. Can a person change their physiological or cognitive characteristics to improve themselves and thus go beyond their own limits?

No decision to perform anthropotechnics can be made during a mission. It is a modification of the body that must be performed prior to the mission, even before the training periods. It is a critical decision because it is irreversible, and can only be made if there is a strong interest in it for a specialized military unit. Consequently, the type of units that could make use of it is open to debate.

5.4.1 Anthropotechnics for Sensory Performance Enhancement

The idea here is to enhance the sensory abilities, mainly vision, but also hearing. For example, to give a better visual acuity without any side effect, by increasing the soldier's capacity beyond their natural limits.

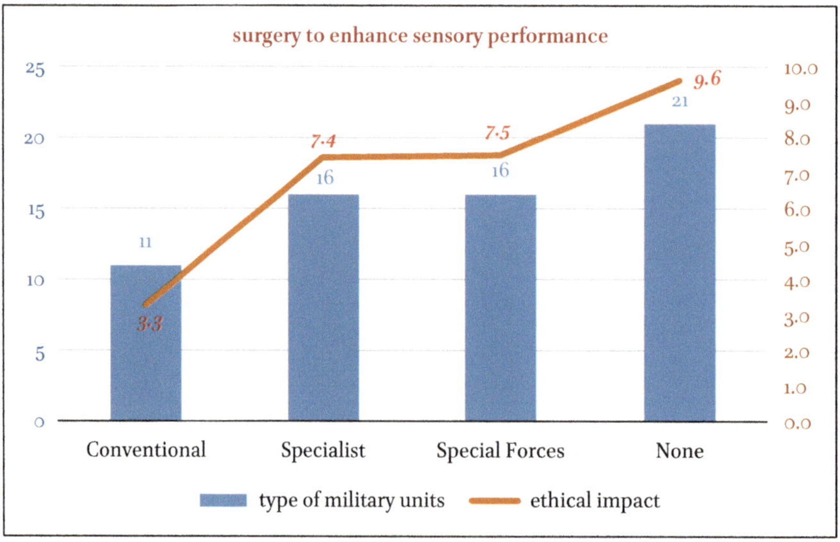

FIGURE 3.13 Ethical impact for performing surgery to enhance sensory performance and for which type of military unit

The question was: in what context do you think the use of surgery for enhanced sensory performance is justified? Examples: eye and ear surgery for improvement (enhancing visual and/or hearing acuteness)

As regards sensory performance enhancement by surgery, a third are against, but two thirds consider it possible for regular or specialized units. Current eye surgery, now fully accepted while once banned by the medical community, is presumably one reason for such results. The more frequently surgery of this type is performed under control of the medical community, the more easily we can imagine that approval will be facilitated.

5.4.2 Anthropotechnics for Sensory Physical Enhancement

Same idea as above except that it concerns physical capacities and no longer sensory capacities. That is to say greater muscular strength for example.

The question was: in what context do you think the use of surgery for enhanced physical performance is justified? Examples: Improving and non-repairing muscle and bone surgery.

Looking at the graph, we go one step further here. 45% reject modification of the human body in view of physical performance. We are here very probably in a deformed vision of humanity, with a soldier who will no longer be completely human.

In a general way, anthropotechnics to enhance senses is better perceived than enhancing the physical body.

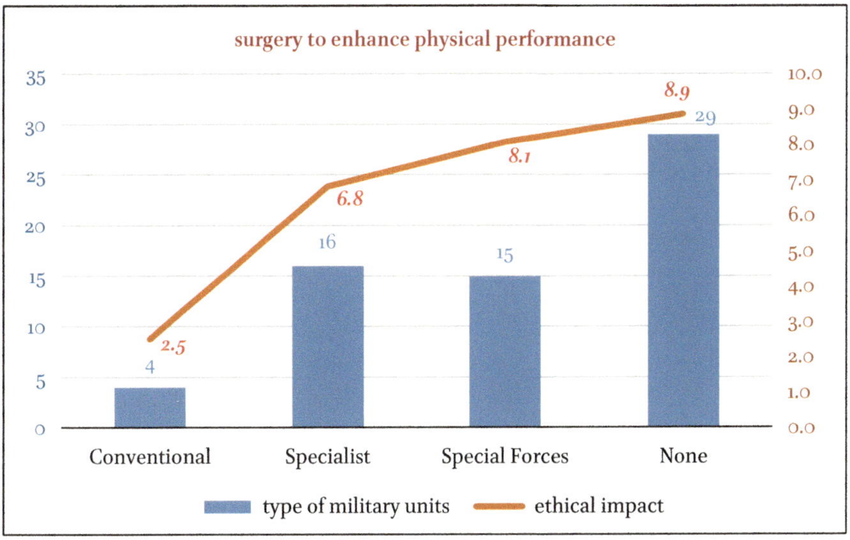

FIGURE 3.14 Ethical impact for performing surgery to enhance physical performance and for which type of military unit

5.5 *Category: Genetics*

The dream of the Nazi superman: a man with a perfect genetic code or an improved genetic code! This is the ethicists' nightmare: is it conceivable for the human species? At least in a military context for better operational efficiency?

5.5.1 Reading the Genetic Code

The idea here is to know the intimate details and abilities of a soldier, and to be able to determine, with the help of the reading of his genetic code, their potential or their weaknesses, with two particular aims: to select one candidate with the best potential but also to prevent potential disease outbreaks for that person.

In this case, we do not modify the genetic code, we only read it.

The question was: In what context do you think the use of genetic analysis to detect potential abilities and risks related to a deficiency of the combatant's genome is justified?

Even for the detection of potentials and capacities, almost half the people are against the use of genetic code reading techniques (around 45%). But the rest still think that it may be an opportunity to keep a constant level of health for soldiers trained for long periods of time, and contribute to an anticipation of any problems that may arise in a soldier's life.

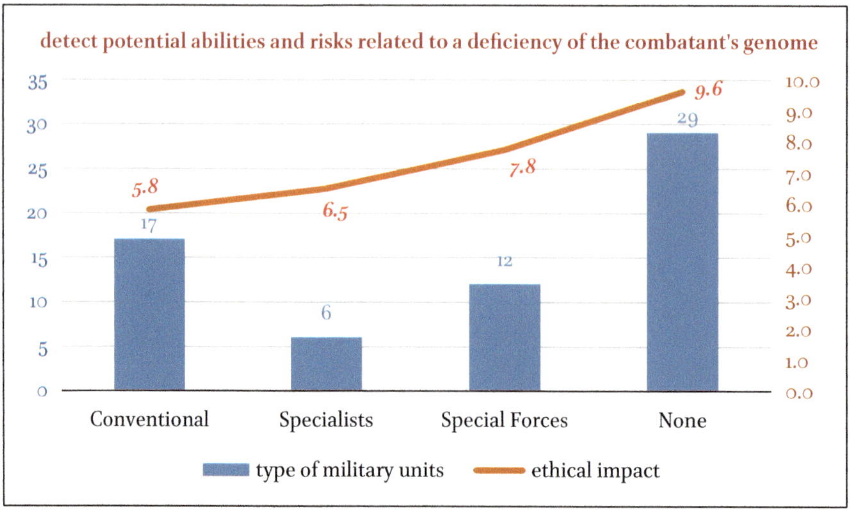

FIGURE 3.15 Ethical impact for detecting combatant's genome potential deficiency and for which type of military unit

5.5.2 Epigenetics and Code Reading

We consider here the possibility of promoting the expression of certain genes or preventing their expression by adapting the soldier's environment (food, training, environment etc.); this is epigenetics.

The question was: In what context do you think it is justified to use epigenetics to enhance the abilities or maintain the health of the combatant without changing the genetic code?

Strangely, the results compared with the previous curve are more tempered, despite the fact that there is no epigenetics without reading the genetic code. The fear is that epigenetics will reveal the fragilities of a person through their genomic code. Therefore, the ethical concern is high.

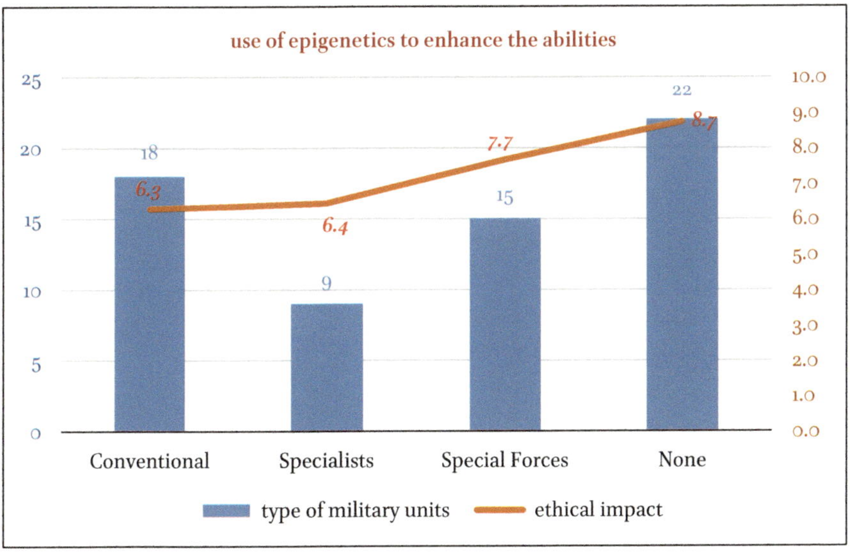

FIGURE 3.16 Ethical impact for using epigenetics and code reading and for which type of military unit

5.5.3 Genetic Manipulation

The most critical question for the individual is: for prevention purposes, or for enhancement purposes, can we change what a person is deeply, what a person's bodily reality is? Because a person is not just a machine determined by their genetic sequencing.

In this question, the issue of transmission of genetic manipulation has not been addressed. We therefore exclude it from the discussion here, considering that genetic modification for the purpose of enhancement should never be transmissible.

The question was: in what context do you think that genetic manipulation to enhance the abilities or preserve the health of the combatant is justified?

Unsurprisingly, a majority of people are against it. Nevertheless, more than a third consider it for conventional or SF units, probably for health reasons more than efficiency.

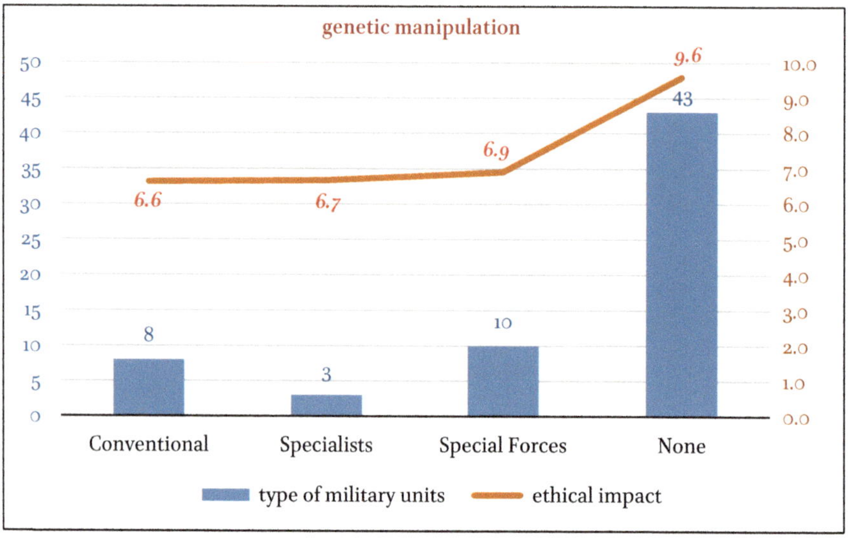

FIGURE 3.17 Ethical impact for performing genetic manipulation and for which type of military unit

6 Differences in Perception of the Ethical Impact According to Professional Categories

This chapter addresses the differences in perception of the ethical impact, according to professional categories. As a reminder, 1 means no ethical impact, and 10 means very high critical issues.

6.1 *Technologies for Acquiring New Skills*

As regards equipment worn by the combatant (Exoskeleton, intelligent clothing), soldiers are more concerned (3.9/10) about their use than medical officers (1.4/10).

Concerning cognitive interfaces (BCI), academics are the most concerned (5.8/10) about the use of this type of equipment, and medical officers are least concerned (3.2/10).

Concerning cognitive stimuli, academics are the most concerned about the ethical impact (6.9/10), one point higher than soldiers (5.4), who are themselves one point higher than medical officers (4.4/10).

6.2 *Pharmacology*

Academicians are the least favourable (between 6.1/10 and 7.2/10) and medical officers are the most favourable in the area of pharmacology (4/10 to 4.4/10). For academics and soldiers, the ethical impact rate is getting high on that point.

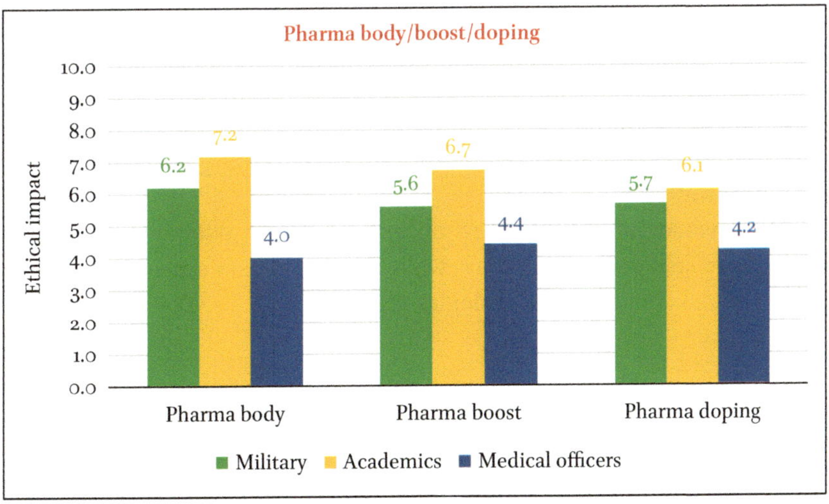

FIGURE 3.18 Differences in perception of the ethical impact for pharmacology per professional categories

6.3 *Implants*

We note here that academics are still the most concerned about the subject of implants, followed closely by soldiers. Medical officers are less suspicious, except for hybridization.

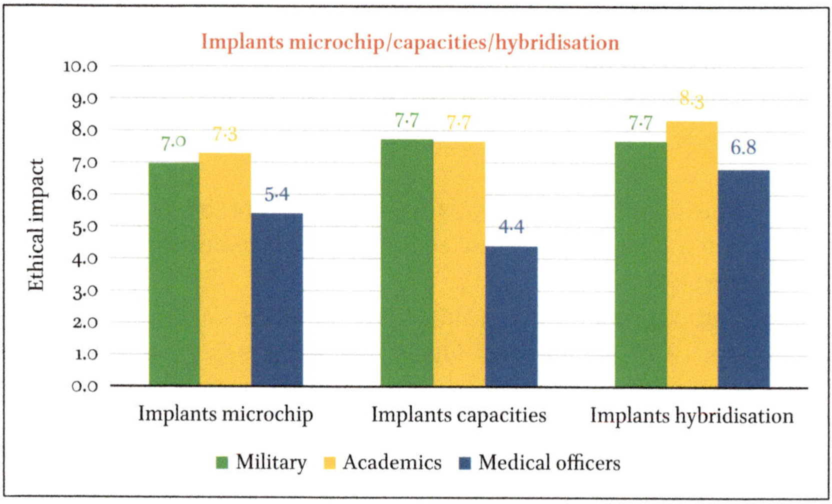

FIGURE 3.19 Differences in perception of the ethical impact for implants per professional categories

6.4 *Anthropotechnics*

There are few differences in the assessment of ethical risk between the three different professional categories. The ethical concern is very high for all, around 7.8 on average.

6.5 *Genetics*

Once again, we see here that medical officers are more confident in these technologies than soldiers or academics, while remaining very much aware of the high ethical risk that these technologies involve.

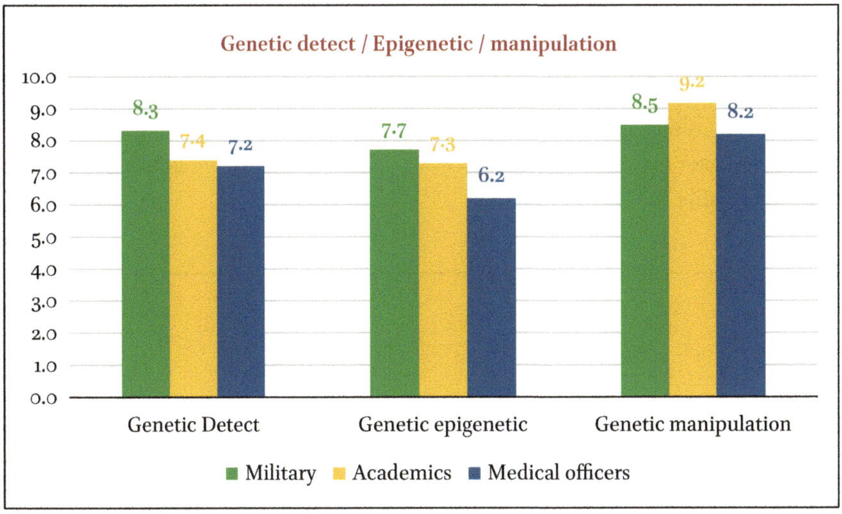

FIGURE 3.20 Differences in perception of the ethical impact for genetics per professional categories

7 Differences in Perception According to European Countries

In order to find trends across European countries, we chose to organize them according to geographical or cultural proximities that seemed relevant to us, depending on the number of responses per country. This choice is of course subject to debate, but we propose it like that. Please note that due to the much higher number of French responses, we have created a French group of its own.

- FR: France (20)
- AS: (Anglo-Saxon): USA, UK, Canada, Netherlands (15)
- EP: Spain, Portugal (6)
- GER: (Germanic) Germany, Austria, Belgium, Switzerland, Finland, Sweden (13)
- SLA: (Slavic) Russia, Serbia, Ukraine, Greece, Hungary, Poland, Czech Republic (8)
- *Note: 2 people did not complete their nationality*

7.1 *Technologies for Acquiring New Skills*

Concerning equipment worn by the combatant (Exoskeleton, intelligent clothing), it can be observed that the Germanic and Anglo-Saxon countries are more favourable than the other groups of countries to this type of equipment. (Ethical impact lower than 4/10). On the contrary, the Slavic countries are the least favourable.

France	AS	EP	GER	SLA
4.1	2.7	3.67	2.93	4.88

For cognitive interfaces (BCI), the Anglo-Saxon countries are in favour of BCI, followed closely by the Germanic countries, although both groups of countries consider the ethical impact to be moderate (5/10). However, the ethical impact estimated by Spain and Portugal is the lowest on this question (3.8/10). The Slavic countries are the most reticent about BCI, with a moderate ethical impact and a minimum mission-at-risk context.

France	AS	EP	GER	SLA
4.25	4.87	3.83	5.07	4.63

Concerning cognitive stimuli, Spain and Portugal are the most favorable from an ethical impact point of view (3.2/10), considering it should only be used for Special Forces. The Slavic countries are the least inclined to this technology, with a moderate ethical impact of (6.3/10). However, like France, they think that it can be used for specialized units. Finally, the Anglo-Saxon countries are rather favorable (conventional units), while the Germanic countries, with an almost identical ethical impact (5.2/10), consider that it can be used mainly for special forces.

France	AS	EP	GER	SLA
5.3	5	3.2	5.2	6.3

7.2 *Pharmacology*

Generally speaking, all countries give the same level of ethical risk for the use of pharmacology, between 5.2 and 6.8.

However, there are two exceptions to this analysis: the Anglo-Saxon countries are much more open to doping techniques than the others, recommending them for all missions; conversely, France is not very favourable to pharmacology affecting physical capacities, only for survival.

7.3 *Implants*

Countries are generally not very supportive of implants, with an ethical concern that is getting high or very high (between 5.5/10 and 8.5/10) and approve for high-risk or even survival missions.

Concerning microchip implants: Spain and Portugal stand out, considering the ethical impact of microchip implants moderate.

France	AS	EP	GER	SLA
7.2	7.1	5.5	7	7

As well as for *Capacities implants*:

France	AS	EP	GER	SLA
8.1	7.4	6.5	7	7.3

And for *Hybridisation*:

France and the Germanic countries are the least favourable to hybridization, with a high ethical impact and in case of survival only. Anglo-Saxon countries are more favourable, with use if missions are risky, despite a higher ethical impact (8.5/10).

France	AS	EP	GER	SLA
8.1	8.5	6.2	7.2	7.9

7.4 *Anthropotechnics*

While countries generally consider that these soldier improvements can be achieved on Special Forces, the ethical impact is relatively high (6.2/10 to 8.3/10). The ethical impact for these two questions for France is the lowest, while paradoxically French respondents are against.

Anglo-Saxon countries as well as Spain and Portugal are quite favourable to surgery to improve sensory on specialized units, but consider the ethical impact very high.

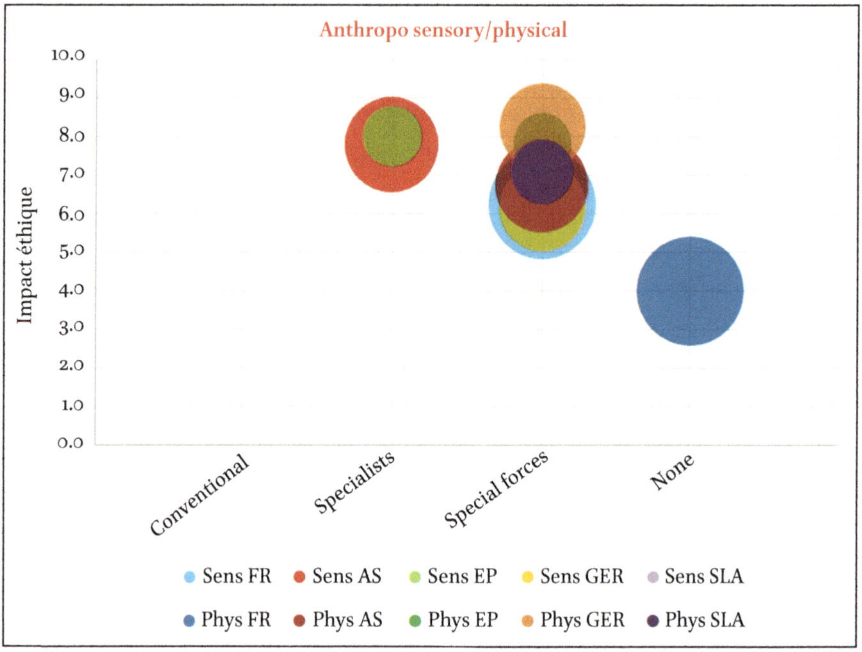

FIGURE 3.21 Differences in perception of the ethical impact for anthropotechnics per countries

7.5 *Genetic*

7.5.1 Reading the Genetic Code

Concerning genetic detection by reading the genetic code, we see a disparity between countries: the Slavic countries are the most in favour of detecting potential assets or risks by reading the combatant's genome, with a relatively low estimated ethical impact (5.4/10), and preferably for specialized units.

On the other hand, France is clearly against, with a very high estimated ethical impact (8.8/10).

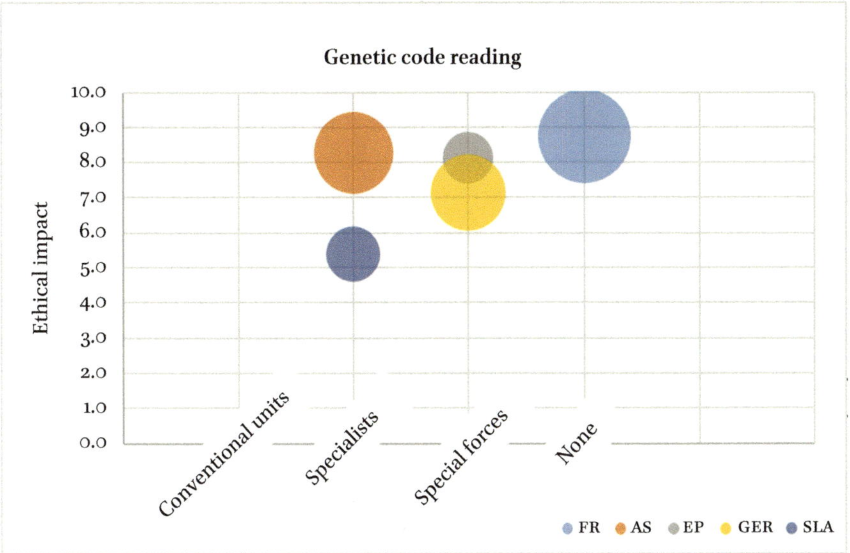

FIGURE 3.22 Differences in perception of the ethical impact for genetic code reading per countries

7.5.2 Epigenetic

France	AS	EP	GER	SLA
7.6	7.8	7.5	7.6	7.6

In general, the use of epigenetics to enhance capabilities is considered to have a high ethical impact (from 7.5 to 7.8/10). France remains formally against, while the Germanic countries as well as Spain and Portugal consider a possible use for Special Forces. The Slavic and Anglo-Saxon countries consider it preferable for specialized units.

7.5.3 Genetic Manipulation

France	AS	EP	GER	SLA
8.4	9.2	8	9.7	7.5

Unsurprisingly, no country is in favour of genetic manipulation, except for the Slavic countries that consider the ethical impact slightly less than the others (7.5/10) and feasible only for Special Forces.

8 Safeguards Regarding Combatant Enhancement

In this survey, it has also been proposed to rate between 1 and 10 (1 = not necessary, 10 = imperative) different safeguards that could serve as a basis for a possible European ethical charter on enhancement.

The proposals stem from previous studies conducted by the CReC Saint-Cyr in its research program on the augmented soldier, as well as from certain recommendations issued by the French Defence Ethics Committee in 2020:

1. No enhancement should be unnatural: "natural" means here that the augmentations do not give the soldier capacities that are not already the property of the human species (*Being nocturnal, for example, is an ability that exists in nature, but which is not present in humans*);
2. No enhancement should dehumanize the soldier;
3. No enhancement should be irreversible;
4. Any enhancement must be validated by the political authority;
5. Any enhancement must be validated by the military medical corps;
6. Any enhancement must be validated by staffs (with a view to meeting military requirement);
7. Any enhancement must be validated by the consent of the individual;
8. No enhancement must ever infringe on the free will of the soldier if it affects the responsibility of the combatant;
9. No enhancement must ever infringe on the free will of the soldier if it allows remote control of the soldier;
10. No enhancement must ever infringe on the free will of the soldier if it downgrades respect for the opponent and dehumanizes combat;
11. No enhancement must ever infringe on the free will of the soldier if it increases his aggressiveness by making him lose his self-control;

12. No enhancement must ever infringe on the free will of the soldier if it disassociates him from his brothers in arms;
13. No enhancement must ever be detrimental to the soldier's personal balance if it affects the soldier's structural integrity (body/mind/soul);
14. No enhancement must ever be detrimental to the soldier's personal balance if it causes the individual to regress in some abilities for the enhancement of others;
15. No enhancement must ever be detrimental to the soldier's personal balance if it induces adverse effects upon return to civilian life;
16. No enhancement must ever be irreversible without the consent of the individual, society, the Armed forces, and the agreement of medical officers;
17. No enhancement must ever be transmissible to others.

The question was: in general, do you think it is necessary to implement the following limitations: give a rate on a scale from 1 to 10 (1 = not necessary, 10 = imperative).

The results show that most of the limitation or safeguard proposals listed here have been validated by the respondents of the survey, with an approval rate of more than 9 out of 10.

Nevertheless 3 proposals are less unanimous than the others with a rate below 8:

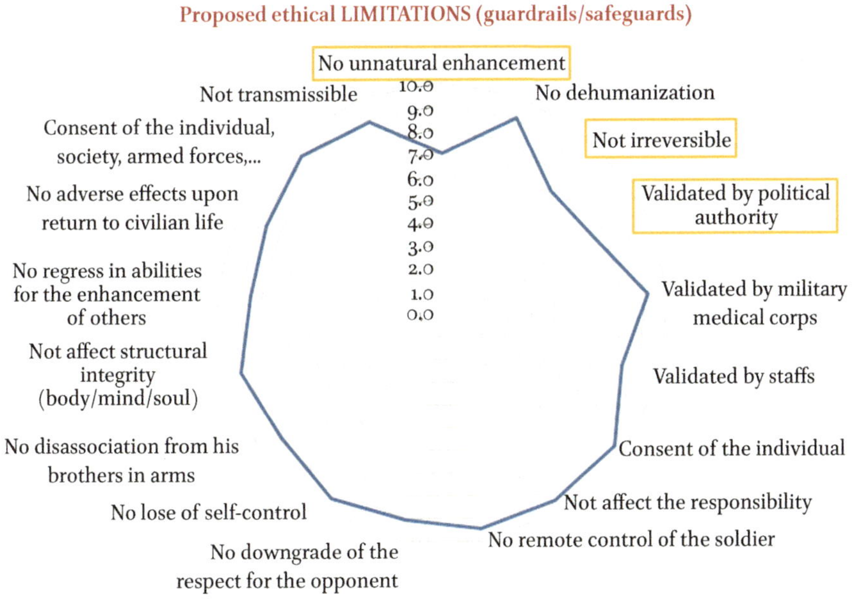

FIGURE 3.23 Rated recommended ethical limitations for soldier enhancement

- First of all, the enhancements which would give a "non-human" perception of the person: this point is difficult to explain and would require further research to understand people's perceptions of this ethical principle of limitation, whose idea is to remain within the limits of human nature.
- The fact that any increase must be validated by the Political Authority: this is probably related to the perceived risk that transparency will limit opportunities of enhancement. Because the Political Authority will never take any risk or will approve enhancement only with so great administrative constraints that it will be unfeasible.
- The fact that it must be reversible!

9 Looking Back at Another Survey Conducted at Saint-Cyr in 2020

M. Axel Augé and the author of this article, both researchers at the Saint-Cyr Military academy research centre, conducted a survey in 2020 with 228 cadets and 45 military officers from this academy.

This survey focused on "the relative acceptability of technical augmentation of the physical-cognitive performances of the combatant". The results have been published in the journal "Tétralogiques" [5].

Below are listed the three main general trends emerging from this survey:

- Firstly, unlike men, women across the questionnaire show greater restraint towards enhancement techniques.
- Second, young military trainees are more likely to accept invasive enhancement than those with more training and operational experience ... It appears that with experience, soldiers learn to know their bodies and their limits, and to manage themselves accordingly, and thus be more easily inclined to face difficulties.
- Thirdly, the singularity of contact units: Infantry, Armoured Cavalry and Combat Engineering. These units focus on raw operational efficiency and are less likely to abandon hardiness and reliance on the intrinsic capabilities of the human body for the potential effects of implants or substances. Having developed fortitude through contact, they have confidence in themselves and their abilities. These contact units have proven operational experience and retain some pragmatism in the field and a strong sense of sacrifice.

10 Some Highlights of This Survey

The data set collected by this study is vast and may be difficult to read. Data show wide inter-personal variety, and differences in appreciation of ethical issues depending on each person.

Nevertheless, some specific features emerge from our analysis:
- trends of the curves are similar for most of the countries;
- a non-zero percentage of those surveyed (6%) are totally against the very concept of enhancement;
- Military personnel with operational experience are generally less likely to favor enhancement;
- Medical officers (8%) surprisingly hardly ever rejected any form of enhancement;

As the sample of respondents seems characteristic of different European sensitivities, it appears to us that this survey is representative at European level and can be used as a reference for further studies.

11 Conclusion

The aim of this survey was to show the diversity of possible forms of combatant enhancement, and to analyse how they are perceived today by soldiers or academics from different European countries. Its ultimate objective is to initiate a debate among the European ethicists and within the military community, which can feed future research work among EuroIsme members.

Even if technology is sometimes ahead of its time, we can be one step ahead and think now how future enhancement techniques that may have direct effects on the combatant could be framed by law and ethical rules.

Work has already been done on this topic; it was published in a book edited by CReC and EuroIsme in 2019 [4]. It highlighted salutary invariants that are non-negotiable and must prevent any use of enhancement. They are reminded here:
- No infringement on free will;
- No attack on the person's psychological balance;
- No enhancement must ever be performed if the moral integrity of the soldiers is downgraded.

We hope that this study will contribute to the continuation of the research work, and that it will give rise to a common debate within EuroIsme in the years to come on this important subject.

References

For more details on the figures displayed, please contact the author at the email address: gerard.de-boisboissel@st-cyr.terre-net.defense.gouv.fr

1. MCDC, *Human Performance Optimization and Enhancement* (22 march 2021).
2. UK ministry of Defence, *Human augmentation: the dawn of a new paradigm* (May 2021).
3. *Opinion of the Defence Ethics Committee on the augmented soldier* (Dec 2020) https://www.defense.gouv.fr/salle-de-presse/communiques/communique_le-comite-d-ethique-de-la-defense-publie-son-avis-sur-le-soldat-augmente.
4. Gérard de Boisboissel, Magdalena Revue, *Enhancing soldiers: a European ethical approach* (October 2019).
5. Axel Augé, Gérard de Boisboissel, *L'acceptabilité relative de l'augmentation technique des performances physico-cognitives du combattant. Enquête auprès des élèves-officiers et de leurs cadres aux Écoles de Saint-Cyr Coëtquidan*, Tétralogiques N°25, La déconstruction du langage (2020). http://www.tetralogiques.fr/spip.php?article157.

CHAPTER 4

Capacity-Increasing Technologies and the Problems of Informed Consent

Jean-François Caron

1 Introduction

Requesting other human beings to use an invasive technology or medicines is by no mean an easy task from an ethical perspective. The Covid-19 pandemic has indeed revealed the numerous challenges connected with this reality to the very vast majority of us, namely: what constitutes informed consent? What are the sorts of emergencies that can justify the accelerated approval and use of a technology/medicine? Are people facing a real choice when their refusal entails important consequences on their career or their livelihood? If these questions were quite new for most of us, members of the armed forces have been exposed to them for a very long time. We can think in this regard of members of the US-led coalition who participated in the liberation of Kuwait in 1991 and who were administered medicines that were still in their "investigational' stage of development"[1] or of US Air Force pilots who must consent to the use of "go-pills" (amphetamines) whenever they are flying extremely long missions at the risk of being grounded. For the first time in their lives, many civilians (not all, of course) who accepted reluctantly to take the Covid-19 vaccines[2] experienced what many soldiers around the world are feeling when they are deployed in war zones, that is not enjoying a genuine right to consent to what they wish to do with their body knowing that their refusal could result in an interdiction to travel, to be allowed in many "non-essential" places or to a termination of their job contract. This is in a nutshell the reality members of the armed forces are facing since refusing these medicines or technologies would result in their incapacity to pursue their career within the organization or would seriously

1 According to the Food and Drug Administration, an investigational drug is a medicine used in clinical investigation. At the time these drugs were administered to soldiers, neither had been studied in a formal clinical trial and no manufacturer was conducting studies.

2 Jean-François Caron, *Irresponsible Citizenship: The Cultural Roots of the Crisis of Authority in Times of Pandemic* (Peter Lang 2021); Jean-François Caron, *The Great Lockdown: Western Societies and the Fear of Death* Peter Lang 2022).

 | DOI:10.1163/9789004544314_006

damage their prospects of future promotion.[3] Therefore, this raises the question of informed consent which simply cannot be assessed independently from the consequences associated with a refusal to comply. When these factors are taken into account, the genuine questions people may have about the reliability and safety of technologies or medicines are overshadowed by the fears associated with them saying "no". As a consequence, if consent is flawed by the numerous factors that can interfere with it, it may be necessary to think of another way behind the development and use of technologies/medicines within the military: a question that is destined to gain more importance with the ever-growing number of capacity-increasing technologies being developed and used in the military.[4] In this chapter, I will argue that the idea of soldiers' consent in the military ought to be replaced with the obligation on the part of the military institution to display a genuine sense of paternalism that can only manifest itself in the manner with which these technologies are being tested and developed.

2 Flawed Consent

The horrifying experiments performed by Nazi doctors in concentration camps had a major influence in the development of medical ethics. Following the war, the Nuremberg Code was established and was composed of 10 main principles that were later reaffirmed in the 1964 Declaration of Helsinki. One of them was the principle of "informed consent" which lies upon the respect for patients' autonomy and self-determination and their ability to willfully decide if they want to receive a medical action without being pressures in any way to do so by others. In order to make that choice a genuine one, physicians are expected to fully disclose the known benefits and potential adverse outcomes of the treatment to the patients who, in return, will then be able to trust the

3 For instance, in the case of the US Air Force, pilots who are refusing to take go-pills are grounded. Anyone who remotely knows the military system is aware that pilot grounding – whatever the circumstances – can have serious implications on someone's career. As a result, this policy tends to put indirect pressure on a pilot to take the pills, even if he technically has the option to refuse using such drugs.

4 Jean-François Caron, *La guerre juste: les enjeux éthiques de la guerre au 21ème siècle* (Les Presses de l'Université Laval 2015); Jean-François Caron, *A Theory of the Super Soldier: The Morality of Capacity-Increasing Technologies in the Military* Manchester University Press 2018); Jean-François Caron, *Contemporary Technologies and the Morality of Warfare: The War of the Machines* (Routledge 2019); Jay Galliot & Mianna Lotz (eds.), *Super Soldiers: The Ethical, Legals and Social Implications* (Routledge 2015).

medical professional. Lastly, it is expected that patients are free to withdraw their consent at any time. As mentioned earlier, the question of "not being under duress" when consenting to a medical treatment or participating into an experiment is open to debate. Indeed, what constitutes an undue pressure by a third party on an individual's choice to perform or not a specific action? We can resort to a restrictive definition by arguing that it is only when saying "no" will likely result in the killing of the patient by another person[5] or we can also use a less restrictive approach that will consider how the consequences of refusing the treatment will negatively impact the individual. The Covid-19 pandemic has shown that refusing vaccine inoculation came with numerous impacts that basically forced individuals to bypass their free will. Indeed, when someone's career is at stake or when there are open threats on the part of politicians about the fact that a special tax will be imposed on the unvaccinated we can indeed wonder if this is not clearly a form of duress and a way to indirectly force vaccination on people. Based on the difference between those who had their required number of doses not to be treated as second class citizens from those who opted to receive booster shots, we can easily conclude that a significant number of people did something against their will and there is ground to be critical about that type of pressure put on people.[6]

If we can be critical at the way politicians have dealt with the Covid-19 pandemic, we also ought to be with the way the military institution throughout the world has ignored soldiers' informed consent following World War II and has treated them as guinea pigs. In this regard, it is possible to recall the numerous nuclear tests carried out by the Soviet Union which exposed thousands of soldiers to radiation. The most famous is certainly the Totskoye exercise undertaken in 1954, which saw an army of 45,000 soldiers march through the epicenter, soon after the nuclear blast of 28 kilotons of TNT. After the collapse of the Soviet Union, documents obtained from the secret military archives stated that these men were exposed to high radioactivity for an extended period of

5 Jean-François Caron, *Disobedience in the Military: Legal and Ethical Implications* (Springer 2018).

6 As of July 2022, 82.9% of Canadians were "fully vaccinated" or had received their "primary course", e.g. at least 2 shots of the Pfizer, Astra Zeneca or Moderna vaccines or 1 dose of the Johnson & Johnson vaccine. This definition prevented those who had fulfilled these expectations from losing their jobs or from seeing their freedom of movement limited (until June 2022, those who were not fully vaccinated could not board a plane, train or boat in Canada). However, the percentage of Canadians who had received at the time additional doses felt to 56.3% (1 additional dose) and to 52% (2 additional doses). Numbers were similar in the European Union where 72.8% had received their primary course of vaccines against 53% who had received 1 booster shot.

time without any protective gear against radiation. The purpose of the exercise was to determine whether troops could fight a battle in an area immediately after it was hit by an atomic bomb. At the time this information was disclosed, about a thousand former Soviet soldiers who took part in the test were still alive and, according to them, they never received adequate treatment for the various health problems they suffered in the aftermath of their exposure.[7]

However, complete disregard of soldiers' health is not solely restricted to inhumane or totalitarian regimes. In this regard, we can think of the various atmospheric nuclear tests conducted by the United States – such as Operations Plumbbob, Castle Bravo, or Crossroads – during which thousands of soldiers were deliberately exposed to radiation.[8] The consequences on the US servicemen who were exposed to these nuclear explosions were devastating for their health. For instance, reports have shown that participants in nuclear experiments have a greater risk of suffering from diseases of the digestive system, particularly cirrhosis of the liver, cancer of the digestive organs. It is also possible to mention Project Shipboard Hazard and Defense conducted in the 1960s by the US Army. This project was a large effort to analyze how sailors aboard military ships could detect and respond to chemical and biological attacks, while maintaining their fighting capacities. On 46 occasions, the servicemen were exposed, without their consent, to numerous chemicals, such as nerve gases VX and Sarin, and other toxic chemicals as well as a variety of biological agents.[9]

Great Britain also famously tested a highly dangerous nerve gas on more than three thousand four hundred guinea pigs from 1945 until 1989 at Porton Down, a place once described by a Whitehall official as 'a sinister and nefarious establishment'.[10] Test subjects were exposed to high doses of Sarin in order to determine how this chemical would impair the mental performance and intellectual capacities of soldiers. The repercussions of this gas were terrible. Between 1952 and 1953, six soldiers were hospitalized as a result of exposure to nerve agents, and another – leading aircraftsman, Ronald Maddison – died on May 6, 1953 after his forearm came into contact with two hundred milligrams

---

7 Marlise Simons, 'Soviet Atom Test Used Thousands As Guinea Pigs, Archives Show' *The New York Times* (New York, 7 November 1993).

8 In total, the United States conducted 1,054 nuclear tests (by official count) between 1945 and 1992, including 216 atmospheric tests.

9 William Blum, *Rogue State: A Guide to the World's Only Superpower* (Zed Books 2006) 152–154.

10 Rob Evans, 'The Past Porton Down Can't Hide' *The Guardian* (London, 6 May 2004).

of pure Sarin.[11] In 2004, a British tribunal ruled that the serviceman was "killed unlawfully".

If these examples are highly condemnable and clear breaches of how informed consent ought to be applied, we can also perceive the numerous ways with which duress may influence soldiers' choices into agreeing against their will to an experiment or treatment that is very similar to what civilians have faced during the Covid-19 pandemic. The fear of dying (which can easily be exaggerated) is one of them. Indeed, just like other human beings, soldiers are led by a strong instinct of self-preservation, and we can assume that many of them will blindly take an advantage, by any means, that would allow them to improve their immediate chances of survival on the battlefield. This point can be highlighted through the experience of former *Luftwaffe* bomber pilot Horst Freiherr von Luttitz who confessed using Pervitin during World War II (the ancestor of crystal meth that was distributed by the German armed forces in industrial quantities to its members after noticing its propensity to increased vigilance, resistance to fatigue, and a sense of invincibility, but that nonetheless caused terrible side-effects) as a necessity and a matter of survival. He said: "Of course you don't abstain from Pervitin because it "might have minor adverse effects on your health. Not when you could die at any moment anyway".[12] Decades after the Second World War, the same logic is also a constitutive reason why American pilots still use go-pills during some of their flights. Lukasz Kamienski writes in this regard:

> During extremely long sorties, which at times continue for more than 40 hours, pilots have no choice, despite officially having the right to choose freely. They are aware that if they do not want to fall asleep or make an error due to enormous operational fatigue, in other words, if they want to return to their base safely, then in specific circumstances they should – for their own sake – resort to stimulants.[13]

Furthermore, the fear of being seen by one's brothers-in-arms as a potential liability to them is also exercising a form of pressure on soldiers who may be reluctant on accepting a technology or drugs. More precisely, if a soldier refuses to

---

11 Ulf Schmidt, 'Cold War at Porton Down: Informed Consent in Britain's Biological and Chemical Warfare Experiments' (2006) *Cambridge Quarterly for Healthcare Ethics* 15(4).

12 'Pervitin, la pilule de Goering', Arte Documentary 2015. https://www.youtube.com/watch?v=1BHxWrZYlSI.

13 Lukasz Kamienski, *Shooting Up: A Short History of Drugs and War* (Oxford University Press 2016) 270.

use them, not only would he increase his own vulnerability, but that exposure could also make his comrades more likely to be harmed. In other words, the fear of protecting oneself from the potential ill-effects of drugs and vaccines in the military might actually lead to situations where members of a unit would have to proceed to a dangerous evacuation on the battlefield, thereby creating a situation that would increase their exposure to death. Considering the camaraderie and the ties that unite soldiers, we can assume that they would nonetheless refuse to use their right to refuse the use of capacity-increasing technologies. As argued by Michael Frisina:

> The success of small unit tactics depends upon unit members being able to perform their assigned tasks when called upon to do so. Unprotected soldiers suffering injury from chemical and biological agents become liabilities to the welfare of their unit members when they are unable to perform their assigned role. Ultimately, the success of the overall mission is potentially jeopardized. If there is a derived benefit from taking these investigational agents and some members fail to accept this benefit, the negative effects of biological and chemical weapons not only impacts on those members not protected but degrades the capability of the entire unit and ultimately the welfare of the other unit members.[14]

The same argument was made by Patrick Lin, Maxwell Mehlman and Keith Abney for whom "The flip-side of consent is refusal to consent, and warfighters are likely to be reluctant to refuse to use a performance enhancement if they think that this would adversely affect other members of the unit, for example, by placing on them more risk or more of the responsibility for carrying out the mission".[15]

Lastly, consequences of refusal on future promotions within the military can also be interpreted as a form of duress on soldiers, such as US Air Force pilots who will be grounded for not accepting to use go-pills: an indelible note in their file that may prevent their future progress in the organization. From this perspective, in a situation where the military encourages (sometimes through the fear of punishment) its soldiers to take medicine as the best way to increase

---

14 Michael E. Frisina, 'Medical Ethics in Military Biomedical Research. Textbooks of Military Medicine: Military Medical Ethics' in Vol. 2. Office of the Surgeon General, Department of the Army, 551.

15 Patrick Lin, Maxwell J. Melhman and Keith Abney, *Enhanced Warfighters: Risk, Ethics, and Policy* (The Greenwall Foundation, 2013 http://ethics.calpoly.edu/Greenwall_report.pdf) 74.

their chances of survival on the battlefield or of not being a liability for their comrades, we can easily presuppose that their "free and enlightened consent" is significantly altered. Consequences on deployments during wartime may also hinder soldiers' consent. For instance, at the infamous Edgewood Arsenal, the US Army tested various chemical substances on more than 5,000 soldiers[16] over a period of 20 years. This is where psychotropic and hallucinogenic drugs such as PCP, LSD, or 3-quinuclidinyl benzilate – commonly known as BZ – were tested to create operational weapons that could incapacitate enemy soldiers.[17] Not only were soldiers lied about the nature of the experiments and their dangers, but many of them were coerced into participating after they expressed second-thoughts by being threatened to be deployed in an active conflict zone. These incentives undoubtedly had a major influence on soldiers' decision to participate freely in the experiments performed at Edgewood. Of course, such explicit threats are unacceptable. This is why the US Army has imposed rules that are supposed to eliminate pressure from superiors.[18] Despite this mechanism, we can nonetheless assume that there is a difference between the theory and the reality of the armed forces. Even with the best intentions, the army will remain a coercive institution that encourages conformity, loyalty, and above all, obedience.

This of course raises serious concerns, namely if individuals who have been pressured in such ways to take medicines or use specific technologies

---

16 These kinds of experiments were preceded by many others. As examples, in 1942, the US Army and Navy doctors infected inmates at a Chicago prison with malaria to study the disease in hope of developing a treatment for it. The prisoners were not told that they were going to be infected with malaria. Nazi doctors used this experiment at the Nuremberg Trials to defend what they did in concentration camps. The US Army also tested mustard gas on four thousand soldiers in 1942. The experiments made use of Seventh Day Adventists who chose to become human guinea pigs rather than serve on active duty.

17 James S. Ketchum, *Chemical Warfare Secrets Almost Forgotten: A Personal Story of Medical Testing of Army Volunteers during the Cold War (1955–1975)* (Bloomington, Indiana: Author House 2012); Raffi Katchadourian 'Operation Delirium' *The New Yorker* (New York, 17 December 2012).

18 The US Department of Defense rules state that 'unit officers and non-commissioned officers (NCOs) are specifically restricted from influencing the decisions of their subordinates to participate or not to participate as research subjects'. It also states that 'unit officers and senior NCOs in the chain of command are required to be absent during research subject solicitation and consenting activities' (US Army, Human Research Protection Office). Finally, participants need to be informed that 'participation is voluntary, that refusal to participate will involve no penalty or loss of benefits to which the subject is otherwise entitled, and that the subject may discontinue participation at any time' (US Army, 1989, Reg. 15-2 I/11/89).

that may tempter with their physical or psychological capacities can be held legally responsible for the criminal acts that may be the direct result of their use or inoculation. Can we consider that soldiers taking capacity-increasing technologies because of the aforementioned implicit pressures are entirely morally responsible for the eventual collateral damages associated with their use? Because of them, are soldiers able to retain their capacity and duty to disobey unlawful orders or are they altering in some way this faculty?[19] Yet, even though they are offered the possibility to consent or not to their use, the case could be made that this choice was not entirely free. A good example in this regard is certainly the use of go-pills used in the US Air Force. These amphetamines do not directly intend to decrease soldiers' moral judgement and increase their sense of obedience. On the contrary, the use of this drug is strictly a matter of military effectiveness as a way to let pilots fulfil their mission and also to increase their chances of survival by making sure that they will stay alert for the whole duration of their flight. Since fighting a war is not a 9 to 5 job, soldiers must remain alert for unusually long periods of time as a matter of survival for themselves, but also for their comrades who they are protecting from the sky. For instance, in Afghanistan, the average soldier in a combat mission was only getting four hours of rest a day; sleep deprivation is the single largest factor in reducing combat performance. Not only are tired soldiers less physically able to fight and run, they also make more mistakes operating complex weapons systems at their disposal – mistakes that can prove deadly to themselves and their comrades. What is seen as a necessity by the military was probably best exemplified by a comment made by Colonel Peter Demitry, Chief of the Air Force Surgeon General's Science and Technology division, who said, "When a civilian gets tired, the appropriate strategy is to land, then sleep. In combat operations when you're strapped to an ejection seat, you don't have the luxury to pull over".[20]

However, the use of this type of medicine is not without unintended risks, as the Tarnak Farm incident that occurred near Kandahar in 2002 has shown. On that fateful night, an American F-16 dropped a five hundred pounds bomb on Canadians who were conducting a night firing exercise, which resulted in the death of four soldiers. The investigation found that the pilot violated

19 Jean-François Caron, *Disobedience in the Military: Legal and Ethical Implications* (Springer 2018); Jean-François Caron, 'Exploring the Extent of Ethical Disobedience Through the Lens of the Srebrenica and Rwanda Genocides: Can Soldiers Disobey Lawful Orders?' (2019) *Critical Military Studies* 5(1).

20 Lianna Hart 'Use of Go Pills a Matter of Life and Death, Air Force Avows' *Los Angeles Times* (Los Angeles, 17 January 2003).

established procedures and his letter of reprimand stated that he flagrantly disregarded a direct order, exercised a total lack of basic flight discipline and blatantly ignored the applicable rules of engagement. In this case, go-pills were directly mentioned as a factor that could explain the pilot's decision, who was ending a 20-hour workday. It was reported that two hours before the incident, the pilot took a 10 mg dose of dextroamphetamine, and his defense attorney stated that the Air Force had pressured his client to take this pill, which, he argued, may have impaired the pilot's judgement.[21]

Although the hearings that followed this tragic incident did not attribute the friendly fire to amphetamines, the pilot nonetheless blamed the incident on the use of these drugs taken following orders from his superiors. Once again, we will never know whether the use of these types of amphetamines – which have side effects, such as confusion, delusions, or auditory hallucinations – were central elements that contributed to this incident. For the sake of argument, let us assume that the use of go-pills indeed affected the pilot's judgement. In such a scenario, how should we determine his responsibility for the deaths of the four Canadian soldiers? On the one hand, it would be possible to argue that it is absolute since he had the choice to refuse to use these stimulants, but, because of all the implicit pressures previously mentioned, there are reasons to believe that he was pressured to take these amphetamines. This begs the question of whether such a pressured soldier should be sanctioned or not? Would it be fair to do so? What could be the possible repercussions on *jus post bellum*?

The inherent problems of obtaining a truly informed consent from soldiers (which is flawed because of the different forms of pressures that can prevent soldiers from refusing a certain medicine) then ought to lead us to think of another way of assessing the proper use of capacity-increasing technologies in the military. The display of a proper form of paternalism on the part of the military institution may be an interesting path to consider.

3 Institutional Paternalism

Because there are reasons to doubt that obtaining someone's genuine consent entirely based upon his free will and not through some forms of duress (which can take different forms of course) can ever be achieved, finding a way to use

21 Doug Simpson, 'Air Force Pushed Pilots to Take Amphetamines, Lawyer Says in Friendly Fire Case' *The Detroit News* (Detroit, 2 January 2003).

capacity-increasing technologies in the military in a manner that will not only treat soldiers as ends in themselves (and not as mere means or as expandable goods) as well as in a way that will be respectful of the moral rules of warfare[22] must be done through a different manner. This way implies the capacity to bypass soldiers' consent in using these technologies insofar as they have been tested and developed beforehand in a manner that leaves no doubt about their safety and their capacity to respect the moral rules of warfare. In other words, members of the military must be able to fully trust the process that led leading to the development of these capacity-increasing technologies in a way that will lead them to believe that they will not harm them, but will rather make their duties easier to perform and increase their chances of survival on the battlefield. This is what can be referred to as "institutional paternalism".

This idea implies a total rejection of the way the military has historically treated their soldiers in the way medicines, drugs or weapons were tested on them. Indeed, the past aforementioned experiments at Edgewood or at Porton Down (and elsewhere) have shown how the military institution has lacked in its obligation to care about its members. New ways to affirm and project a renewed and stronger version of paternalism are therefore necessary when it comes to the use of new devices or medicines – elements that are at the core of capacity-increasing technologies.

Strictly from a moral standpoint, the development and use of capacity-increasing technologies can be justified from two perspectives, namely, as a constitutive component of the military's duty of care toward its members and as a way to increase the morality of warfare. Both these elements strongly militate in favor of their use. Needless to say however that these technologies should not be employed on the battlefield if they deprive soldiers of the capacity to disobey unlawful and immoral orders or if they might lead to situations where soldiers could not be held responsible for their actions. This implies that military research needs to find ways that will allow a distinction between technologies and medicines that do not harm these principles from those that do. This can only be achieved through a thorough research and development process that will be respectful of participants' health and safety.

It has already been established that requiring soldiers' consent is not an optimal solution. As a consequence, if consent for the use of medicines and capacity-increasing technologies ought to be waived for members of the armed forces, it implies that they should have full confidence that the military will not

22 Jean-François Caron, 'Defining Semi-Autonomous, Automated and Autonomous Weapon Systems in Order to Understand their Ethical Challenges' (2020) 1 *Digital War* 173.

order them to use things that might be harmful to their health. In other words, the fear that their institution might betray their trust by ordering them to use dangerous technologies for their health must be eliminated.

Only a consequent framework for military research might erase this suspicion that numerous servicemen and civilians might legitimately have. In order to establish such a trusting relationship, the use of technologies and medicines that might increase soldiers' capacities on the battlefield should be the final element of a long process of testing. First, any military research aiming at increasing soldiers' capacities should first pass the stage of animal testing before moving to human testing. At this point, and on the basis of Kantian ethics and an institutional duty of care, participation in these experiments should focus first and foremost on the consequences for the participants' immediate and long-term health. For these scientists, the potential of what they are testing for the achievement of military objectives should never be the prime concern. This could be achieved through the implementation of an ethical committee composed of individuals independent from the military and the chain of command as a way to avoid any possible conflict of interests and to make sure that the priority would be given to the rights of human subjects.

Forms of undue pressure should be minimized as much as possible. In order to make this theory a tangible reality, superior commanding officers should never be present during the experiment, and no mention of a volunteer's refusal to pursue testing should be mentioned in their military file as scientists should not be allowed to report their refusal to any member of the military authorities officially or unofficially.

Such a process is by no means a novelty in the field of military research as it is closely connected with the approach put forward during the Spanish American War, almost half a century before the establishment of the Nuremberg Code. At that time, yellow fever was a threat to US soldiers and outbreaks were so frequent in the Caribbean that it prompted President Theodore Roosevelt to ask the Army Surgeon General, General George M. Sternberg, to create a commission to study this disease and the ways in which it could be treated efficiently. The process of testing medicines on combatants was a milestone in military research at the time, even though it was attacked by antivivisectionists. During his address to the Congress of American Physicians in 1907, William Osler, a physician from Johns Hopkins Hospital and a key member of the Roosevelt commission, stated the importance of animal testing and the voluntary nature of participation in experiments. He stated the following:

> The limits of justifiable experimentation upon our fellow creatures are well and clearly defined. The final test of every new procedure, medical

> or surgical must be made on man, but never before it has been tried on animals. […] For man absolute safety and full consent are the conditions which make such tests allowable. […] Once this limit is transgressed the sacred cord which binds physician and patient snaps instantly. […] Risk to the individual may be taken with his consent and full knowledge of the circumstances, as [has] been done in scores of cases, and we cannot honour too highly the bravery of such men as the soldiers who voluntarily submitted to the experiments on yellow fever in Cuba.[23]

Of course, from a strategic point of view, some might come to believe that these procedures might be harmful to military secrecy that is necessary in order to accomplish military objectives. In the case of a widespread disease like yellow fever, which cannot be used intentionally by an armed force against its enemy, the need for secrecy is not the same as the one associated with the development of a sophisticated new military device or medicine that might procure a strategic advantage. Moreover, it would be a mistake to limit secrecy simply to the need for military dominance. Secrecy is also an essential component of the military's duty of care. While it is difficult to defend a country or win a war if your enemy knows about your strategy, your armaments, technological capacities, or troop movement, it would also increase the vulnerability of soldiers as the enemy would know the Achilles heel of those it is fighting. From that perspective, protecting military technological development becomes a moral obligation as a means to maximize the military's duty of care. In this sense, being open with soldiers who test new technologies or medicines constitutes a risk. On the other hand, the previously mentioned experiments that occurred in the 20th century prove that military secrecy was often used as a formidable way to cover up research so morally corrupt that it abused human subjects and treated them simply as expendable goods. In other words, while it can be deemed a fundamental for preserving soldiers' life, it can also be used as a way to treat them as guinea pigs.

However, one wonders if a balance can be established between the need for secrecy and openness with those who are testing these new technologies as a way to respect their welfare. Given the bond that unites members of the armed forces, stating with insistence that their life and their comrades' well-being depends on their silence might be a strong incentive for them; being threatened with dishonourable discharge or judicial consequences would be also be

23 William Osler, 'The Historical Development and Relative Value of Laboratory and Clinical Methods in Diagnosis. The Evolution of the Idea of Experiment in Medicine' (1907) 7 *Transactions of the Congress of American Physicians and Surgeons* 1.

a good compromise and would not be an unacceptable burden from a moral perspective. In other professional organizations, such as civilians working as civil servants, employees are also subjected to silence over confidential information they might encounter while performing their duties under the risk of facing significant consequences. For instance, in France, jurisprudence has stated that a serious breach of confidentiality can lead to the immediate termination of an employee's contract and, if it can be proven that the employee acted with the intent to harm his employer or to illegally profit from the disclosure of secret information, he exposes himself to a fine and up to three years in prison.

Respecting these guidelines would achieve numerous important goals. More importantly, it would force the military to develop capacity-increasing technologies that will not be harmful to soldiers' health and their sense of responsibility, and would not hamper their right to ethical disobedience. Not only would they be treated with respect and as ends in themselves, but it would also help to preserve the essential morality of warfare and not run counter to the principles of *jus post bellum*. Moreover, knowing that the development of technologies or medicines respects these guidelines, members of the military would have no reason to fear that their employer is not acting out of pure paternalism, but rather for their own good. Accordingly, waiving soldiers' consent for their use would not be as problematic as it may sound.

Of course, respecting these guidelines implies that the military should be seriously pro-active in its research in order to address situations where it has to use untested or unapproved medicines on its members because of an unforeseen threat. This type of scenario, which led, in the aftermath of the 1990–1991 Gulf War, to numerous criticisms and a shared feeling among servicemen and civilians that the military used dangerous products, is less likely to happen again. The problem with such a situation is the uncertainty linked with the use of these types of medicines. Although they might actually increase soldiers' protection on the battlefield, they can also affect their health or moral agency – a risk that can only be assessed months or years after these technologies or medicines have been used. Sometimes, it can already be too late. In the interlude, soldiers' health can be affected forever, individuals can end up losing their moral agency and commit crimes for which responsibility could be very difficult to determine under current judicial principles. The military's duty of care should be a certainty and the use of untested and unapproved technologies creates the possibility of its violation as well as the transgression of moral principles that allows wars to be fought justly. This is why proactivity in research and testing is so fundamental and should be a constitutive element of military research.

4 Conclusion

Overall, the use of capacity-increasing technologies remains morally necessary and an essential component of the military's duty of care, insofar as they are able to increase the safety of soldiers without posing a threat to their health or negatively affect their moral agency on the battlefield. The distinction between acceptable technologies from those that are not can only be made through a long process of experiments and testing. Only such a process could make the necessity of obtaining soldiers' consent superfluous: an obligation which, as I have argued, can be flawed in many ways.

CHAPTER 5

'Green proportionality': *in bello* Ecology in Just War Theory

Dragan Stanar

1 Introduction

It is not uncommon today to hear that somehow time itself has sped up for modern humanity, that changes occur more frequently and more rapidly making it increasingly difficult for us just to keep track. It seems as though every aspect of human existence has been going through constant change in past decades, at a rate higher than ever before. Many of these profound changes are caused by groundbreaking scientific discoveries and technological breakthroughs which ushered us into a truly 'new' age of humanity in which we need to constantly reexamine and reevaluate *everything* we thought we 'objectively'[1] knew about ourselves, human society, nature, and entire existence. Naturally, we are often confused and perplexed when trying to make sense of new phenomena and all of the diffuse implications they have both on our common world and our private lives. The main cause for our evident and growing epistemological anxiety and axiological disorientation in the 'new' world is the widening gap between natural sciences which provide us with the 'instruments … and know-how' to do something and social sciences which give us the answer to the question why and if we should do it.[2] We are faced with many things

1 Perhaps the most prominent characteristic of postmodern world is the negation of all 'objective knowledge' and universal everlasting truths, especially scientific axioms. These characteristics of the post-modern era have deep and sometimes unsettling implications. More in Ilija Kajtez, Dragan Stanar, 'Postmodern thought and modern world' in *Proceedings of the First international conference on sustainable environment and technologies* (UNT 2021) 333–346.

2 At some point in recent history, we decided to use the science-provided *possibility* to do or create something as an *automatic justification* to do or create it. We are today, as humanity, a victim of this false logic by which we do everything we can before actually understanding whether we should do it. Possibility itself is understood as justification. More in: Јован Бабић, 'Наука и стварност' [Science and reality] in Драга Мастиловић (ed.), *Идеја филозофског факултета и савремени универзитет* [Idea of the Faculty of Philosophy and the Contemporary University] (Филозофски факултет Универзитета у Источном Сарајеву 2018) 59.

 | DOI:10.1163/9789004544314_007

that profoundly influence all aspects of our world, things which in fact have no clear justification for their existence. We are therefore forced to seek solutions, alter and conform our laws, norms, and customs in order to eliminate, or at least hinder, their devastating implications and effects, especially when they concern our planet and our only natural habitat.

2 The Changing Nature of War and Military Ethics

As an intrinsic attribute of human civilization, war remains, and will remain, our reality as long as civilization exists. This cataclysmic form of human conflict does not exist in a vacuum – it also changes, transforms and almost evolves along with human society. Therefore, war and its 'practical nature', is also undoubtably rapidly changing, perhaps even 'too rapidly', due to the same abovementioned factors that cause all changes: scientific revelations, technological advances, unstoppable and relentless progress of information and communication innovations, global political and economic transformations, modifications of basic cultural matrix, etc. However, this transformation of war includes more than just alterations of its 'military aspects', i.e., new weapons, tactical, operational and strategic changes, etc., but, in certain aspects, also changes of its very nature, meaning and logic.[3] Naturally, military ethics must adapt and evolve along with the phenomenon which has pivotal significance for this field of practical or applied ethics;[4] ideally, both military ethics and the nature of war change and 'evolve' at the same pace. Changes in military ethics should therefore optimally reflect all changes in warfare, the use of armed forces, our understanding of the phenomenon of war, its political meaning, etc.

However, military ethics must also be expanded and tailored in such a way that it adapts to and accommodates not only the changes in the character of war *stricto sensu*, but the key paradigmatic global and civilizational shifts likewise, even if they *prima facie* have nothing or little to do with war. Actually, one

---

3 Martin van Creveld, *Transformation of War* (The Free Press 1991); Срђан Старчевић, Срђан Благојевић, 'Кревелдов спор са Клаузевицем – да ли је смисао рата политички' [Creveld's Argument with Clausewitz – is the meaning of war political?], (2017) 56(2) *Српска политичка мисао* 117–134.

4 'Military ethics, as a field of applied ethics, does not deal solely with war, but war remains its central notion and the area of primary interest' Драган Станар, *Праведан рат – између апологије и обуздавања рата* [Just War – Between Apology and Restrain of War] (Добротољубље 2019) 10.

of the most profound characteristics of war that makes it so central to human history is that it is affected by all dimensions of society while it simultaneously affects all segments of it, even if certain parts of society are 'not interested in war'. Our considerations of what is permitted, what ought to be done, and especially what ought not to be done and what is forbidden in war, cannot be isolated and cut off from the overall comprehensive dispositions of modern humanity and our global *zeitgeist* which dictates our current essential civilizational values, goals, and aims.[5] These elements do not 'change' the phenomenon of war *per se*, but they do radically change our *perception* of war and our *attitudes* on actions and practices in war.

If we were to identify one dominant global movement, some would say even mainstream global political ideology, that is affecting virtually all spheres of human civilization today, it would indeed be ecologism. Ecologism (environmentalism, ecopolitics, climate politics or green politics) places utmost significance on preservation of our environment, the 'non-human world', which is more than worth of profound moral consideration. This comprehensive political ideology aims to protect the environment and non-human nature at all costs, via creating completely new, or amending and reshaping the existing key economic, political, legal, cultural and all other social norms. Military ethics, an area of applied ethics which deals with moral norms concerning armed forces, particularly in the context of war, must surely also at least analyze its existing theoretical and practical premises and propositions in order to examine if they in fact aid and contribute to the noble cause of ecologism and preservation of our natural habitat. However, military ethics must remain very cautious of potential ideological blindness and distortion of reality and truth, which inevitably come with all ideologies and seem to be inherent to all of them, including ecologism.[6]

3 Ethics of War and Ecology

Despite there being several entirely and radically different ethical perspectives on war,[7] it seems that military ethics predominantly, and quite expectedly,

5 It goes without saying that universal moral norms remain unaffected and unaltered by the *zeitgeist*, especially when considering the morality of war and warfare.

6 The danger lies in potential and not unimaginable scenario in which military ethics, under the powerful ideological influence of ecologism, places 'our' environment over lives of 'their' people, paving the way for theoretical justification of large-scale killing in war.

7 Usually, we differentiate between three main ethical perspectives on war: pacifism, realism and JWT. These perspectives or traditions are not homogenous, as there are numerous

focuses on the Just War Theory (JWT). JWT, due to its complexity and extensiveness perhaps better referred to as Just War Tradition, represents a 'pragmatic compromise'[8] between two dialectically opposed extreme views embodied in pacifism and realism. Over the course of more than 15 centuries, JWT evolved into an elaborate and comprehensive system of though and ideas concerning each and every aspect and 'phase' of war. Therefore, modern JWT comprises of four distinct elements, each concerning a (chronologically) different aspect of war – *jus ante bellum, jus ad bellum, jus in bello* and *jus post bellum*.[9] For the purpose of our research, we shall focus on the element of JWT most relevant, most important and basically fundamental for military ethics – *jus in bello*.[10]

Jus in bello is the element of JWT which relates to the moral judgment of warfare, i.e., ethical evaluation of actions and decisions during war and combat. As such, it comprises of 'normative attitudes on what it is permissible to do in war'[11] and thus directly concerns military members and all combatants. As a separate and coherent concept within JWT, *jus in bello* began to be shaped in the 16th century, by the thinkers belonging to the famous School of Salamanca who created the concept of *debitus modus*,[12] or the just manner of waging war. Contemporary *jus in bello* norms, rules, and restrictions, which apply equally to all combatants, regardless of the justness of their side in war,[13] are formulated via two key criteria – discrimination and proportionality. Despite it traditionally

---

diverse and specific views on war. However, 'there are very few theories in ethics of war which can resist ultimately being placed in one of these traditions' Брајан Оренд, 'Рат' [War] in Драган Дулић, Бранко Ромчевић (eds.), *Етика рата* [Ethics of War] (reader, Факултет безбедности 2010) 270.

8 David Whetham, 'Just War Tradition: A Pragmatic Compromise' in David Whetham (ed.), *Ethics, Law, and Military Operations* (Palgrave MacMillan 2011) 68.

9 More on Just War Theory, each of its elements and their mutual relationship in Станар (n 4).

10 All other elements of JWT, especially its most prominent one, i.e., *jus ad bellum*, do not fall into the realm of military ethics as much as they do in the field of political ethics.

11 Nicholas Rengger, 'The *Jus in Bello* in Historical and Philosophical Perspective' in Larry May (ed.), *War: Essays in Political Philosophy* (CUP 2008) 33.

12 Suarez coined the phrase *debitus modus*, while de Vitoria explicitly separated the justness of war (*jus ad bellum*) from justness in war, or the issue of '*Quantum liceat in bello justo*' (how much is permitted in a just war), as he formulated it. Gregory M. Reichberg, 'Just War and Regular War: Competing Paradigms' in David Rodin, Henry Shue (eds.), *Just and Unjust Warriors* (OUP 2008) 199.

13 Classical, Walzerian, understanding is that *jus in bello* must remain separated from *jus ad bellum*, and that 'war must always be judged twice' Walzer (n 5) 21. However, in the last decade or so, some revisionists (Jeff McMahan and David Rodin being the most prominent) asserted that we cannot fully separate our moral judgment of actions in war from the moral status of war. Jeff McMahan, *Killing in War* (Clarendon Press 2009).

not being a part of *jus in bello,* the legal principle of military necessity[14] conveniently and usefully supplements the two criteria in discussions on warfare. While the principle of discrimination (distinction, selectivity) prescribes and differentiates legitimate from illegitimate targets, i.e., combatants from non-combatants, the criterion of proportionality, *inter alia,* primarily considers the magnitude and type of force used in military actions against legitimate targets. So, is there any place for ecological considerations in *jus in bello*?

3.1 *'Green Proportionality' in* jus in bello

Having in mind the previously asserted thorough and all-encompassing global significance of ecologism for modern human civilization, significant place must be made for ecological considerations in *jus in bello,*[15] as it has become painfully clear that modern wars cause grave damage to the 'non-human world' as well as to our dimension of existence. The two worlds, non-human and human, do not exist independently and they cannot be separated from each other as we are destined to live in the 'natural world', the only habitat we have, while the 'non-human world' continues to suffer and undergo seemingly perpetual modifications at the hands of the dominant species, as there is 'little to no human action that does not have an effect, to one degree or another, on some aspect of the environment'.[16] Our individual lives, our cultures, and the entire human civilization are inextricably entangled with and shaped by our natural environment while possibly the most important trait of human kind is our ability and proclivity to profoundly alter, adapt, and manipulate nature to our ideas and needs.[17] Therefore, it would not only be erroneous and naïve, but also extremely foolish and irresponsible to exclude consideration of nature and our non-human environment from the moral analysis of such a tremendously and critically vital phenomenon for humanity – war.

---

14 More on the position and role of military necessity, and the reason it is often neglected in traditional JWT in: Eric Patterson, 'Military Necessity, Proportionality, and Discrimination: The Case of Veracruz' in Dragan Stanar, Kristina Tonn (eds.), *The Ethics of Urban Warfare* (in print, Brill Nijhoff 2022) 106–125.

15 We can also argue that such considerations perhaps can even be necessary in all other elements of contemporary JWT, especially in *jus ad bellum.*

16 Kirsten Stefanik, 'The Environment and Armed Conflict: Employing General Principles to Protect the Environment' in Carsten Stahn, Jens Iverson, and Jennifer S. Easterday (eds.), *Environmental Protection and Transition from Conflict to Peace: Clarifying Norms, Principles, and Practices* (OUP 2017) 93.

17 Many a philosopher, even some of the most famous ones, saw man's triumph over natural determinism and conquest of nature itself as our *differentia specifica.*

The context of war reveals an unfortunate implication of our essentially inherent interconnection with nature – almost all things[18] belonging to the 'non-human world' basically were, are and will continue to be considered legitimate targets in war, as long as their destruction rationally contributes to our military goals and hinders our enemy's war effort. The *in bello* principle of discrimination or selectivity will therefore almost certainly continue to 'justify' targeting 'nature'[19] in cases in which it actually impedes our enemy's efforts, under the excuse of military necessity, especially when the 'damage to the environment is an unsought consequence of the achievement of some other objective, such as the impairment of an enemy's ability to produce weapons'.[20] This, of course, does not mean that self-evident restrictions should not continue to be applicable, as targeting certain elements of nature (clean water, natural food sources, etc.) or using certain classes of weapons clearly cannot be justified and are and should in fact be considered as *malum in se*.[21] However, the second *in bello* principle, criterion of proportionality, can and in fact must be expanded and supplemented in such a way that it explicitly includes meaningful ecological considerations as 'even when targeting admittedly legitimate military objectives, there is a need to avoid excessive long-term damage to ... natural environment'[22] Contemporary understanding of *in bello* proportionality in JWT is such that it 'limits the quantity and quality of force used against combatants with the military advantage gained',[23] meaning that the advantage must justify the force used to gain it.[24] But, in this process of measuring

18 There are, of course, certain things that are considered to be unjustifiable in war, such as 'the ancient and despised crime of poisoning the well' Brenda Almond, 'The Ethics of Virtue vs the Ethics of Justice' (*The Independent*, 13th of May 1999) https://www.independent.co.uk/arts-entertainment/the-ethics-of-virtue-vs-the-ethics-of-justice-1093404.html.

19 Not only targeting the 'non-human world' explicitly, but also those elements of the 'human world' whose destruction directly contributes to the destruction of nature and the environment.

20 Aaron Schwabach, 'Environmental Damage Resulting from NATO Military Action Against Yugoslavia' (2000) 25 (117) 139.

21 In JWT, some acts in war are considered to be *mala in se,* i.e., evil in itself, and can thus never be justified by any amount of utility they produce. These acts include rape, ethnic cleansing, genocide, poisoning of food and water sources, etc.

22 *Final Report to the Prosecutor by the Committee Established to Review the NATO Bombing Campaign Against the Federal Republic of Yugoslavia* (1999) 1, 18.

23 Драган Станар, *Етика међународне политике* [Ethics of International Politics] (Добротољубље 2021) 321.

24 A common mistake pinpointed by Rodin is that proportionality requires 'similarity in the forcefulness of the means utilized by defender and aggressor' Aside from being unrealistic, such requirement would be irrational. David Rodin, *War and Self-Defense* (Clarendon Press 2004) 115.

and weighing, it is usually only the 'harm that an act of war would cause to civilians'[25] that is taken into account. In this sense, according to Rodin, proportionality only considers 'loss of civilian life, injury to civilians, damage to civilian objects, or a combination thereof'[26] when weighting it against military advantage. Even in its broadest iteration,[27] there is no requirement to consider ecological consequences of military actions in the *in bello* proportionality calculus.

The concept of 'green proportionality' represents an attempt to broaden the principle of *in bello* proportionality so it would take into consideration not only military and civilian casualties and damage caused by a military action, but also its effects on the environment when weighting and justifying gained military advantage. Our generation's wars, and particularly our weapons of devastating destructive power, capable of total annihilation of both 'worlds' (human and non-human), accentuate the necessity of introducing such a concept into moral deliberation of warfare – virtually every military in the world is capable of causing large-scale and long-lasting desolation of the environment, either by using nuclear, biological, radiological and chemical weapons or by targeting facilities and installations whose destruction causes immense pollution and contamination of nature. The analysis of the ongoing war in Ukraine will surely further prove this contention, as the theatre of war is pervaded with locations which have the potential of becoming major pollutants and ecological disasters. However, the war in Ukraine is raging as we speak, so to say, and the objective reality of war is covered by a thick opaque epistemological *Nebel des Krieges*,[28] so characteristic and inherent to every modern war. We shall have to wait until the war ends and we reach a safe historical distance at which

---

25 McMahan (n 14) 20.

26 David Rodin, 'The Moral Inequality of Soldiers: Why *jus in bello* Asymmetry is Half Right' in David Rodin, Henry Shue (eds.), *Just and Unjust Warriors: The Moral and Legal Status of Soldiers* (OUP 2008) 53.

27 Several authors insist that proportionality must also take into account the lives and suffering of combatants, not just non-combatants, and demand 'the least possible amount of killing and suffering, as a parameter of the lowest possible cost of war. Jovan Babić, 'Etika rata i teorija pravednog rata' [Ethics of war and just war theory] in Petar Bojanić, Jovan Babić (eds.), *Asimetrični ratovi i teorija pravednog rata* [Asymmetric wars and just war theory] (Akademska knjiga i Institut za filozofiju i društvenu teoriju 2017) 196.

28 The notion 'fog of war' is usually used to describe a complete lack of certainty during military operations for all participants. Moreover, the entire war as a phenomenon is enshrouded by this fog which impedes all efforts to analyze events, even by impartial and objective parties. Extensive propaganda efforts, constant mutual accusations, false flag operations, the neoteric fake-news phenomenon, and outright fabrications make it practically impossible to *in bello* analyze modern wars while they last.

this epistemological fog will, at least minimally, dissipate and allow us to critically analyze events and actions of both sides, including those relevant for a 'ecological perspective' of war. Nonetheless, we can apply our proposed 'green proportionality' reasoning to one of the most recent wars in Europe which caused substantial ecological destruction.

3.2 *'Green Proportionality' in the NATO Bombing of Yugoslavia*

During the NATO bombing of Yugoslavia in 1999, the country was intensely bombed for 78 days causing 'damage to the environment', according to the official *Final Report to the Prosecutor by the Committee Established to Review the NATO Bombing Campaign Against the Federal Republic of Yugoslavia*.[29] In the course of the bombing campaign, which encompassed all parts of Yugoslavia including the current NATO member Montenegro, many ecologically sensitive non-military objects and installations, which are usually considered to be legitimate targets by JWT,[30] were hit and destroyed. Following the 'classical' *in bello* understanding, these actions were perceived as respectful to both principles – discrimination because they were observed as legitimate targets; and proportionality because combatant and non-combatant casualties of these actions were understood as proportional to the advantage gained.[31] Yet, if we add ecological considerations to deliberation of proportionality, and observe severe and multilayered direct and indirect ecological consequences and environmental effects of such actions, things drastically change. Even if we agree with the arguable assertion that, unlike Vietnam and Kuwait where 'environment itself was a target', in Yugoslavia 'the environmental damage was incidental to the achievement of some other objective'.[32] According to available data, more than 1900 non-military objects were hit in the air-raids, over 400 of which being delicate industrial and energy facilities.[33] Among many targets which caused severe ecological damage, the gravest ecological consequences were produced in bombing the oil refinery in Novi Sad and the industrial complex in Pančevo.

---

29 (n 23) 1, 14.

30 JWT legitimizes targeting objects which contribute to 'arms and logistics' as they represent a 'contribution to the threat' – arms factories, roads, bridges, airports, oil refineries, chemical plants, etc. Thomas Nagel, *Mortal Questions* (CUP 1979) 71.

31 In key incidents we shall discuss in this paper, three non-combatants were killed in Pančevo refinery bombings, while two non-combatant victims were claimed in air-raids targeting the refinery in Novi Sad.

32 Schwabach (n 21) 118.

33 Spasoje Smiljanić, *Agresija NATO na SRJ* [NATO Aggression on Yugoslavia] (Vesti 2012) 70–73.

The oil refinery in Novi Sad, a city in the north of Serbia, was hit with more than 250 missiles, causing destruction of over 73.000 tons of raw oil. Roughly 90% of oil burned, 9% was spilled on the soil contaminating over 43.000 square meters of fertile soil, while 1% went into the Danube River[34] (Bakrač, Klem and Milanović 2018: 479, 488). The industrial complex in Pančevo, consisting of an oil refinery and two plants for manufacturing mineral fertilizer and petrochemicals, which was hit on 12 different occasions in the month of April alone, leaked out over 9700 tons of ammonia, over 1100 tons of oil fuel, ten tons of rubber, two tons of fertilizer, chlorine, mercury, polyvinyl chloride, vynilchloride monomer, and many other highly toxic compounds and chemicals. According to Schwabach, 'the magnitude of the disaster greatly exceeds, in volume and probably in toxicity, that of Europe's greatest peacetime incident, the 1986 Sandoz warehouse fire in Schweizerhalle, near Basel, Switzerland'.[35] Although the official and controversial Balkan Task Force Report concluded that the 'Kosovo conflict has not caused environmental catastrophe affecting the Balkans region as a whole', it did in fact recognize both Novi Sad and Pančevo, alongside Kragujevac and Bor, as 'environmental "hot spots"'[36] in which environmental contamination was identified.

Based on the findings of the BTF, the previously mentioned *Final Report to the Prosecutor* concluded that 'the environmental damage caused by the NATO bombing campaign does not reach the Additional Protocol I threshold'[37] and as such does not constitute legal liability. This conclusion is quite strange, having in mind not only the objective long-term consequences the bombing had on the environment, the pollution of air, soil, and water, atmosphere, one of the largest European rivers (Danube) and its ichthyofauna, biodiversity and overall population health, but also the fact that the same report recognizes that the 'UNEP study may not be a reliable indicator of the long term environmental consequences of the NATO bombing'[38] as it was concluded only months after the war ended! If we observe the situation after the expected latency period[39] ended in 2005/2006, we would note, among many other extremely alarming things, that the incidence rate and mortality of systemic tumors skyrocketed

34 Saša Bakrač, Emilija Klem, Miško Milanović, 'Ekološke posledice NATO bombardovanja Republike Srbije 1999. godine' [Ecological consequences of NATO bombing of Serbia in 1999], (2018) 7 *Vojno delo* 481.

35 Schwabach (n 21) 119.

36 UNEP/UNCHS Balkan Task Force (BTF) Situation Report (1999) 10–11.

37 (n 23) 1, 17.

38 *Ibid.*

39 Latency period signifies the period between exposure to cancerogenic agent to clinical manifestation of tumors.

by 118% in Serbia and that high levels of pollution still exist, particularly in Pančevo and on the entire territory of Kosovo and Metohija.[40]

The pollution and ecological damage were further amplified by the use of depleted uranium projectiles during the entire campaign. According to a quite conservative estimates provided for the UN by NATO, more than 32.500[41] depleted uranium missiles were fired during air-raids, over ten tons of which was dispersed in the environment.[42] Interestingly, for some unclear and inexplicable reason the *Final Report to the Prosecutor* advised that the 'OTP should not commence an investigation into use of depleted uranium projectiles by NATO',[43] despite the fact that depleted uranium weapons are recognized as 'weapons which can simultaneously threaten both the environment and human health'.[44] Nonetheless, the Italian Parliament established four inquiry commissions over the course of ten years in order to investigate the prolonged effects of depleted uranium missiles on Italian soldiers who spent time in Kosovo, after 366 Italian soldiers died from systemic tumors upon returning from mission.[45] As a result of reports of these commissions which proved that there is a 'direct causal link between exposure to depleted uranium and the pathologies cited by the soldiers',[46] in 2019 the Italian defence minister Trenta announced a new law which would enable military personnel to receive compensation.[47]

If we would today ethically reevaluate many actions of NATO in Yugoslavia, in a sort of a *ex post* proportionality analysis which would include the element of 'green proportionality', we would undoubtably come to a conclusion that

40 Much more alarming data is available. Vladislav Jovanović, Slobodan Petković, Slobodan Čikarić, *Zločin u ratu, genocid u miru* [Crime in war, genocide in peace] (Službeni glasnik, Društvo Srbije za borbu protiv raka 2012).

41 Serbian sources claim that the number is much higher, ranging from 50.000 to 60.000 projectiles.

42 Bakrač et all. (n 35) 479.

43 *Final Report* (n 23) II, 26.

44 Stefanik (n 17) 113.

45 Nicole Corritore, 'Depleted uranium: state crime' (*Osservatorio Balcani e Caucaso Transeuropa,* 9th of May 2019) https://www.balcanicaucaso.org/eng/Areas/Balkans/Depleted-uranium-a-state-crime-194266.

46 Redazione ANSA, 'Law to protect soldiers from depleted uranium' (*ANSA*, 21st of May 2019) https://www.ansa.it/english/news/2019/05/21/law-to-protect-soldiers-from-depleted-uranium-trenta_28aeb7e2-9223-4bc4-a8ee-0c7798e9e86e.html.

47 Tom Kington, 'Italy's defense minister backs links between cancer in military personnel and exposure to toxic uranium' (*Defense News,* 31st of May 2019) https://www.defensenews.com/global/europe/2019/05/31/italys-defense-minister-backs-link-between-cancer-in-military-personnel-and-exposure-to-toxic-uranium/.

they were in fact highly disproportional, taking into account the widespread, severe and long-term damage[48] to the natural environment[49] – not only the devastation of oil refineries and chemical facilities in Novi Sad, Pančevo and other locations all over Yugoslavia, but also the decision to use depleted uranium ammunition. The dire environmental, and indirectly long-term human health consequences and harm of these actions and decisions are exceedingly disproportionate to the military advantage gained by NATO. Even though it is true that it is 'difficult to assess the relative values to be assigned to the military advantage gained and harm to the natural environment'[50] in *ex ante* deliberations, the specific context of the bombing, the constellation of power and sheer risk ratio between belligerent parties made NATO 'well positioned to take environmental concerns into account'.[51] After all, as Schwabach points out, 'the NATO countries were winning, not losing, the air war in Yugoslavia'[52] making it highly improbable that the 'rationally assumed grave environmental harm'[53] could be justifiable by genuine military necessity.

4 Conclusion

Following not only the changes in the nature of war, but also civilizational shifts and headway, military ethics, and with it its central element, i.e., ethics of war, must also adapt, develop, and evolve. The global growing ecological consciousness and the environmentalism movement are changing all spheres of human existence and reshaping reality from top to bottom. War and armed forces are no exception to this. In recent years, we have witnessed some unprecedented developments and heard statements that would sound

48 These notions which constitute the threshold of responsibility for damage, as written in the *Additional Protocol I*, are recognized by many as 'considerably vague and open to conflicting understandings by interpreters'. Carsten Stahn, Jens Iverson, Jennifer S. Easterday, 'Introduction – Protection of the Environment and *Jus Post Bellum*: Some Preliminary Reflections' in Carsten Stahn, Jens Iverson, Jennifer S. Easterday (eds.), *Environmental Protection and Transition from Conflict to Peace: Clarifying Norms, Principles, and Practices* (OUP 2017) 3–4.

49 A thorough systematic review of direct environmental consequences detected in only three years following the NATO bombing of Yugoslavia is available in: Dragoljub Antić, Jasmina Vujić (eds.), *Environmental recovery of Yugoslavia* (Vinča Institute of Nuclear Science 2002).

50 *Final Report* (n 23) I, 19.

51 Schwabach (n 21) 139.

52 *Ibid.*

53 *Final Report* (n 23) I, 22.

completely bizarre only a few decades ago – from recent statement of US president Joseph Biden in which he expects a switch to 'green vehicles' in armed forces and 'climate-friendly military'[54] in the near future, to the now already famous announcement of a major arms producer that its Sea Sparrow anti-aircraft missile is the 'most environmentally friendly'[55] and the official program of the US Department of Defense called 'Green Bullets'[56] which aims to substitute dangerous materials used to produce ammunition with more 'environmental friendly' ones.

International law also recognized, some time ago, the need to adapt to new ecological challenges of warfare. The most important document, *Additional Protocol I to the Geneva Conventions,* already in 1977 in Article 35, explicitly recognizes that it is 'prohibited to employ methods or means of warfare which are intended, or may be expected, to cause widespread long-term and severe damage to the natural environment', while Articles 55 and 56 demand 'Protection of natural environment' and 'Protection of works and installations containing dangerous forces'.[57] In addition, the previously formulated 1976 *ENMOD Convention* prohibits 'Military or any other Hostile Use of Environmental Modification Techniques', while *Resolution 687* of the Security Council defines liability to international law for 'environmental damage'.[58] Finally, voices demanding for a fifth Geneva convention, which would explicitly protect nature in war are becoming increasingly louder.[59]

And while admittedly legal and moral norms 'can hardly be observed as two completely separate and independent wholes',[60] ethics of war is not the same as laws of war. Therefore, military ethics must also critically reexamine the existing JWT, as a philosophical framework for moral discussion of war, and adapt it to reflect the necessary ecological demands, just as international law has been trying to do for decades. Ethical education of military personnel,

54 Josie Ensor, 'Joe Biden unveils plan to make every US military vehicle "climate friendly"' (*The Telegraph,* 22nd of April 2022) https://www.telegraph.co.uk/world-news/2022/04/22/joe-biden-unveils-plan-make-every-us-military-vehicle-climate/.

55 RaytheonTech official Twitter account (31st of August 2021) https://twitter.com/RaytheonTech.

56 Ken Swarmer, 'Army's "Green" Ammo' (Military, 2022) https://www.military.com/history/armys-green-ammo.html.

57 ICRC, *Additional Protocol I to the Geneva Convention* (1977) Articles 35, 55, 56.

58 Stahn et all. (n 49) 2.

59 Jonathan Watts, 'Make environmental damage a war crime, say scientists' (*The Guardian,* 24th of July 2019) https://www.theguardian.com/law/2019/jul/24/make-environmental-damage-a-war-say-scientists-geneva-convention.

60 Dejan Stanković, 'Moral i pravo u savremenoj pravnoj filozofiji' [Moral and law in contemporary legal philosophy], (2001–2002) XIX–XX *Filozofija i društvo* 204.

officers in particular, must incorporate ecological and environmental considerations into the study of ethics of war. One of useful and important steps in that overall direction must surely be the addition of 'green proportionality' in the *in bello* moral calculus of war. The 'non-human' world, i.e., its destruction and the aftermath of it, must also be deeply considered when weighing direct military advantage secured in a particular operation against the damage inflicted by force used – both in the context of target and weapons selection *and* both from an anthropocentric and naturalistic perspective.[61] Utilitarian moral calculus, which is predominantly used in military ethics, in this context must also pay special attention to long-lasting ecological consequences of military actions, through careful consideration of several utilitarian variables, such as Purity and Extent[62] of the effect of a military action. Probabilities of negative effects of an action creating utility and regard for the number of people affected by both cannot be ignored when weighing military advantage against ecological damage.

61 Naturalistic perspective aims to 'protect the environment *per se*' while the anthropocentric perspective values nature as human environment and only possible habitat.

62 The 'father' of utilitarianism, Jeremy Bentham, includes Purity, Fecundity and Extent in his moral utility calculus, along with Fecundity, Intensity, Duration, Certainty and Propinquity.

CHAPTER 6

On the Juxtaposition between Privacy and Excellence; Ethical Considerations Regarding Data-Collection during Recruitment for Military Missions in the 21st Century

David William Mac Gillavry and Zdeněk Mikulka

Over the past decades, the emphasis in military operations has began to shift from large-scale engagements between conventional forces to precise, almost surgical actions, performed by highly-trained specialists.[1] Although this tendency has certainly been aggravated by both technological advancement and financial restrictions (maintaining a large standing army is more resource-intensive than smaller, but better trained and equipped forces), it probably has its roots in increasing political pressure to limit both losses and collateral damage. Ever since the Vietnam war, which is widely regarded as the first televised conflict,[2] the horrors of war have been beamed straight into the living rooms of ordinary citizens (e.a. voters) and, consequently, modern wars are fought out almost as much in the public information sphere, as they are on the battlefield. This tendency has, especially with the advent of social media, picked up steam in recent years and the pressure on modern militaries, at least in liberal democratic states in which information dissemination is relatively free, thus mounts to conduct operations at increasing levels of accuracy and professionalism. In an age where one image of an injured child, who got caught in the crossfire, can turn public sentiment against a military mission, excellence amongst frontline soldiers, rather than brute force, is becoming an increasingly decisive factor in the outcome of military engagements.

Modern militaries can meet this public demand for excellence in part through the implementation of more effective training protocols and tactics,

1 Steven P Bucci, 'The Importance of Special Operations Forces Today and Going Forward' [2015] Index of U.S. Military Strength; Stephen Biddle, 'Special Forces and the Future of Warfare : Will SOF Predominate in 2020 ?' 22.

2 Tony Maniaty, 'From Vietnam to Iraq: Negative Trends in Television War Reporting' (2008) 14 Pacific Journalism Review 89; Michael Mandelbaum, 'Vietnam : The Television War' (1982) 111 Daedalus 157.

 | DOI:10.1163/9789004544314_008

as well as through the adaptation of new technologies. Precision-guided munitions, drones and devices that aid target recognition, such as night vision equipment, all play an undeniable role in the mitigation of collateral damage. However, no amount of technology or protocols can fully eliminate the human factor in combat and, consequently, the moral fortitude, stress resilience and ability to perform under extreme conditions of frontline military personnel ultimately determine the excellence and professionalism of a modern military.

This drive for excellence calls for ever more precise research into detectable markers of both exceptional potential on the one hand, and heightened susceptibility to sub-optimal coping on the other, as well as subsequent screening for said markers in both prospective recruits and, with a certain regularity, in serving military professionals. Technologically, both research into, and screening for, such markers can be achieved with relative ease (a range of physical and psychological tests are already utilised for these purposes, while others such as functional magnetic resonance imaging (fMRI) and electroencephalogram (EEG) testing for a range of neurological anomalies, genetic testing for heightened susceptibility to a range of mental and physical disorders, and heart-rate variability (HVR) tests for stress resilience, to name just a few, are already widely used for research purposes and could easily be adopted for selection procedures as well). However, although the implementation of such technologies could dramatically optimise selection procedures, it would undoubtedly raise questions about the individual's rights to privacy.

Firstly, many of the technologies that could potentially be used to identify relevant physiological markers of excellence require broader testing to be effective, which may reveal a host of information about the individual, which is not directly relevant to the markers tested for, but may, nonetheless, expose certain aspects of the individual's being of which they might prefer to stay ignorant themselves or want the rest of the world to be ignorant of. We will refer to such data as "accidental" data, because it was not part of the original focus of the test and its existence can thus be described as accidental. An fMRI screening, for instance, would be meaningless without a record of anatomical data on the individual's brain. As such, a screening may reveal a host of neuroanatomical anomalies, which the study was not designed to detect. These can range from the detection of potential undesirable growths (e.a a tumorous mass) to neurological markers of specific pathologies. A significant enlargement of the striatum, for instance, has been identified as a neurophysiological feature in psychopathy,[3] whereas increased amygdala volume has been linked to anxiety[4] and a larger nucleus accumbens to obesity.[5]

Secondly, screening for biophysical markers would lead to hard, albeit statistical, data about an individual's natural predispositions. It must be noted, however, that any system under investigation does not exist in a vacuum and it is de facto impossible to predict the behavioural outcomes of any predisposition without reference to the larger interconnectedness of the system for specific individuals.[6] This leads to two serious issues. On the one hand, statistical testing will inevitably dispense with the influence of individual variation and thus effectively nullify personal motivation, conviction and the willingness to press on, regardless of limitations. However, the larger issue, is that, because biological systems are highly interconnected, these data will, consequently, reflect not only on the trait under investigation, but also on a host of unrelated characteristics of the individual, which they might a. want to remain ignorant of, and b. are often of a highly personal and sensitive nature. An fMRI screening may, for instance, be aimed at responsiveness to stressful stimuli in the locus coeruleus (LC), a region in the brainstem, which may indicate the presence of,[7]

---

3 Andrea L Glenn and others, 'Increased Volume of the Striatum in Psychopathic Individuals' (2010) 67 Biol Psychiatry 52; Olivia Choy, Adrian Raine and Robert Schug, 'Larger Striatal Volume Is Associated with Increased Adult Psychopathy' (2022) 149 Journal of Psychiatric Research 185 <https://doi.org/10.1016/j.jpsychires.2022.03.006>; Bariş O Yildirim and Jan JL Derksen, 'Mesocorticolimbic Dopamine Functioning in Primary Psychopathy: A Source of within-Group Heterogeneity' (2015) 229 Psychiatry Research 633.

4 David Hessl and others, 'Fear Potentiated Startle in Children With Autism Spectrum Disorder: Association With Anxiety Symptoms and Amygdala Volume' (2021) 14 Autism Research 450; Jenifer Juranek and others, 'Association between Amygdala Volume and Anxiety Level: Magnetic Resonance Imaging (MRI) Study in Autistic Children' (2006) 21 Journal of Child Neurology 1051.

5 Kristina M Rapuano and others, 'Genetic Risk for Obesity Predicts Nucleus Accumbens Size and Responsivity to Real-World Food Cues' (2017) 114 Proceedings of the National Academy of Sciences of the United States of America 160.

6 Many biological systems, including human neuroendocrine systems (see: Robert Sapolsky and Steven Balt, 'Reductionism and Variability in Data: A Meta-Analysis' (1996) 39 Perspectives in Biology and Medicine.), are non-linear in nature and can thus not be reduced to their component parts; e.a. some of their properties are emergent from the system as a wole but do not reside in any of its component parts (for two excellent works on the non-linearity in natural systems see: Stephen Wolfram, *A New Kind of Science* (1st edn, Wolfram Media, Inc web: 2002); James Gleick, 'Chaos: Making a New Science' 2004.

7 T O'Donnell, KM Hegadoren and NC Coupland, 'Noradrenergic Mechanisms in the Pathophysiology of Post-Traumatic Stress Disorder' (2004) 50 Neuropsychobiology 273; Christoph Naegeli and others, 'Locus Coeruleus Activity Mediates Hyperresponsiveness in Posttraumatic Stress Disorder' (2018) 83 Biological Psychiatry 254; ERS Nijenhuis, O Van

or heightened susceptibility to,[8] post-traumatic stress disorder (PTSD). This would, naturally, be extremely relevant to any military institution preparing to send personnel on mission. However, in addition to elevated susceptibility to PTSD, heightened LC reactivity in response to stressful stimuli has also been associated with a tendency for clinical depression[9] and opiate addiction.[10]

In this paper, we address these issues and raise the question, of when, and under which circumstances, the military's need for excellence supersedes the individual's right to privacy. Especially within the context of frontline military personnel, this question becomes incredibly pressing because of the high-stress/high-risk environments in which military professionals operate and the ready access they have to potentially lethal equipment. This paper is however not intended to provide an answer to this question, but rather to raise a concern that, on our view, will only increase in prominence over the following years.

1 "Accidental" Data; Can It Be Utilised?

We were first confronted with the problem of accidental data when running a relatively routine fMRI study into post-combat PTSD. Most active military personnel, who had combat experience, noted on their informed consent that they did not wish to be informed of any neurological anomalies that might show up on the scans. This was not because of any personal convictions, but simply because they are obligated to inform the military in case of any known

der Hart and K Steele, 'The Emerging Psychobiology of Trauma-Related Dissociation and Dissociative Disorders' (2002) 2 Biological Psychiatry 1079.

8 David Ullrich and David William Mac Gillavry, 'Mini-Review: A Possible Role for Galanin in Post-Traumatic Stress Disorder' (2021) 756 Neuroscience Letters 135980.

9 David Weinshenker and Philip V. Holmes, 'Regulation of Neurological and Neuropsychiatric Phenotypes by Locus Coeruleus-Derived Galanin' (2016) 1641 Brain Research 320; Lauren Jacobson, 'Glucocorticoid Receptor Deletion from Locus Coeruleus Norepinephrine Neurons Promotes Depression-like Social Withdrawal in Female but Not Male Mice' (2019) 1710 Brain Research 82; Qian Zhang and others, 'Locus Coeruleus-CA1 Projections Are Involved in Chronic Depressive Stress-Induced Hippocampal Vulnerability to Transient Global Ischaemia' (2019) 10 Nature Communications.

10 Steven J Grant, Yung H Huang and D Eugene Redmond, 'Behavior of Monkeys during Opiate Withdrawal and Locus Coeruleus Stimulation' (1988) 30 Pharmacology, Biochemistry and Behavior 13; David William Mac Gillavry and David Ullrich, 'A Novel Theory on the Predictive Value of Variation in the β-Endorphin System on the Risk and Severity of PTSD' [2020] Military Psychology 1; Emanuele Claudio Latagliata and others, 'Norepinephrine in the Medial Pre-Frontal Cortex Supports Accumbens Shell Responses to a Novel Palatable Food in Food-Restricted Mice Only' (2018) 12 Frontiers in Behavioral Neuroscience 1.

health issues, which may in turn negatively affect their future careers. A moral issue however arose, when a potential mass was detected near the amygdala in one of the participants. Especially because this brain region is involved in fear processing and aggression,[11] and the individual in question was preparing for his next mission, concerns about both their safety and that of those serving with them rose. Fortunately, in this case, the neurologist on call identified the observed anomaly as an artefact of the fMRI machine, rather than a neurological anomaly and, consequently, the moral dilemma placed before us, was resolved. However, it did raise an important question: what if it had been a mass? Do you make the information known and violate the participant's wishes? Or do you remain silent and risk a potential disaster somewhere down the line?

To complicate matters further, this problem should be understood on two levels. The first, as was our case, relates to research participants. From a formal point of view, at least, researchers are bound by the conditions under which participants agree to participate in a study (usually agreed upon when giving informed consent). Breaching confidentiality, which was part of the preconditions, as pointed out by the participant through noting that they did not want to be informed of any potential issues, would thus seriously compromise research standards and ethics. However, does the formal point of view outweigh the moral obligation one has as a human being to avoid harm to others when one can? Especially if the individual in question will be placed in a high-stress environment, with the means to do serious damage.

In a research environment, this issue can be solved relatively easily by incorporating a clause in the informed consent documentation that outlines that, due to the nature of the participant's profession, certain results will have to be shared with both the individual and their employer. Because participation in research projects is voluntary, this would allow those who do not feel comfortable with this condition, to opt-out of the study. The incorporation of such a clause would limit the number of participants in any study, but it would effectively mitigate the moral issue outlined above.

11 Swantje Matthies and others, 'Small Amygdala High Aggression? The Role of the Amygdala in Modulating Aggression in Healthy Subjects' (2012) 13 World Journal of Biological Psychiatry 75; Jozsef Haller, 'The Role of Central and Medial Amygdala in Normal and Abnormal Aggression: A Review of Classical Approaches' (2018) 85 Neuroscience and Biobehavioral Reviews 34; Justin M Moscarello and Stephen Maren, 'Flexibility in the Face of Fear: Hippocampal–Prefrontal Regulation of Fear and Avoidance' (2018) 19 Current Opinion in Behavioral Sciences 44; Maxwell R Bennett, Sean N Hatton and Jim Lagopoulos, 'Stress, Trauma and PTSD: Translational Insights into the Core Synaptic Circuitry and Its Modulation' (2016) 221 Brain Structure and Function 2401.

A further issue with academic research relates to military-relevant physiological markers of excellence. Whereas the past decades have seen some major advancements, in the identification of potential vulnerability factors for, and indicators of, suboptimal coping, excellence has received relatively little academic attention, and the work done in the field has, in many cases, focused predominantly on philosophical reflections based on personal observation or phenomenological descriptions. Consequently, if hard data are produced at all, these data derive predominantly from studies into the efficacy of said philosophical reflections, rather than from concise hypothesis construction. This becomes abundantly clear in leadership studies, a field which has been plagued with methodological issues.[12] The common response is to acknowledge that rationalist methodologies cannot be applied to complex social phenomena and that, therefore, the field should revert to phenomenological descriptions of individual leadership occurrences. However, such methodologies have been used to great effect in the study of other complex social phenomena, such as religion,[13] art,[14] ethnocentrism and out-group antagonism,[15] and secrecy.[16] Consequently, it stands to reason that the problem in leadership studies lies not so much with the methodologies used as such, but rather with the way they are employed.

As mentioned above, more success has been achieved in the identification of markers of potential vulnerability factors and indicators of sub-optimal coping. Especially where sub-optimal coping commonly leads to clinical diagnoses or may provide deeper insights into the worst of human behaviour, research has

12 Sverre Spoelstra, Nick Butler and Helen Delaney, 'Never Let an Academic Crisis Go to Waste: Leadership Studies in the Wake of Journal Retractions' (2016) 12 Leadership 383; Mats Alvesson and André Spicer, 'Critical Leadership Studies: The Case for Critical Performativity' (2012) 65 Human Relations 367; Sverre Spoelstra, Nick Butler and Helen Delaney, 'Measures of Faith: Science and Belief in Leadership Studies' (2021) 30 Journal of Management Inquiry 300; Mats Alvesson and Katja Einola, 'Warning for Excessive Positivity: Authentic Leadership and Other Traps in Leadership Studies' (2019) 30 Leadership Quarterly 383 <https://doi.org/10.1016/j.leaqua.2019.04.001>.

13 Justin L Barrett, 'Exploring the Natural Foundations of Religion' (2000); Justin L Barrett, 'Cognitive Science of Religion : What Is It and Why Is It ?' (2007) 6 768; Joseph Bulbulia, 'The Cognitive and Evolutionary Psychology of Religion' (2004) 19 Biology & Philosophy 655; Stewart Guthrie, *Faces in the Clouds: A New Theory of Religion* (Oxford University Press 1993).

14 VS Ramachandran, 'Sharpening Up "The Science of Art"' (2001) 8 Journal of Consciousness Studies 9.

15 (de Dreu et al. 2012; De Dreu et al. 2011; Schnall et al. 2008; Vicario et al. 2017)

16 David William Mac Gillavry, 'Rethinking Secrecy in Religion Cognition and the Intimacy of Secrecy' (Brill Academic Publishers, 2018) 301.

been prolific. Research into post-traumatic stress disorder (PTSD), for instance, is moving ever closer to identifying a range of genetic,[17] epigenetic,[18] neuroendocrine,[19] and neurological,[20] markers of heightened vulnerability. Likewise, although it is thus far impossible to make accurate individual predictions, the sociological,[21] psychological[22] and neurological[23] roots of communal violence outside of the rules of engagement (i.e. genocide, unlawful executions, gang rape, etc.) are by now reasonably well understood (see for instance:) [24]

Many of the same issues affect screening for selection purposes. However, where research participation is generally voluntary, the same cannot be said

17 (Duncan, Cooper, and Shen 2018; Duncan et al. 2018; Daskalakis et al. 2018)

18 Karestan C Koenen and others, 'Juvenile Conduct Disorder as a Risk Factor for Trauma Exposure and Posttraumatic Stress Disorder' (2005) 18 Journal of Traumatic Stress 23; Mark W Miller and Patricia A Resick, 'Internalizing and Externalizing Subtypes in Female Sexual Assault Survivors: Implications for the Understanding of Complex PTSD' (2007) 38 Behavior Therapy 58; Erika J Wolf and others, 'Posttraumatic Stress Disorder and the Genetic Structure of Comorbidity' (2010) 119 Journal of Abnormal Psychology 320.

19 Xiongfeng Pan and others, 'Catecholamines in Post-Traumatic Stress Disorder: A Systematic Review and Meta-Analysis' (2018) 11 Frontiers in Molecular Neuroscience; Jacques Dayan, Géraldine Rauchs and Bérengère Guillery-Girard, 'Rhythms Dysregulation: A New Perspective for Understanding PTSD?' (2016) 110 Journal of Physiology Paris 453; Ullrich and Mac Gillavry (n 8).

20 Naegeli and others (n 7); Nijenhuis, Van der Hart and Steele (n 7); Mohammed R Milad and others, 'Recall of Fear Extinction in Humans Activates the Ventromedial Prefrontal Cortex and Hippocampus in Concert' (2007) 62 Biological Psychiatry 446.

21 Christopher Browning, *Ordinary Men: Reserve Police Battalion 101 and the Final Solution in Poland* (Penguin Books 2001).

22 Donald G Dutton, 'The Psychology of Genocide, Massacres, and Extreme Violence: Why "Normal" People Come to Commit Atrocities' [2007] The psychology of genocide, massacres, and extreme violence: Why 'normal' people come to commit atrocities 199; Leonard S Newman and Ralph Erber, *Understanding Genocide: The Social Psychology of the Holocaust* (2002).

23 Hanah A Chapman and Adam K Anderson, 'Things Rank and Gross in Nature: A Review and Synthesis of Moral Disgust' (2013) 139 Psychological Bulletin 300; Hanah A Chapman and Adam K Anderson, 'Understanding Disgust' (2012) 1251 Annals of the New York Academy of Sciences 62; Martin Kavaliers, Klaus Peter Ossenkopp and Elena Choleris, 'Social Neuroscience of Disgust' (2019) 18 Genes, Brain and Behavior 1.

24 Dutton, D. G. (2007). *The psychology of genocide, massacres, and extreme violence: Why "normal" people come to commit atrocities*. Westport, London: Preager Security International; Mac Gillavry, D. W., Mikulka, Z., & Stříbrný, J. (2023). On the Cognitive Science of Communal Taboo-Breaking Behaviour. Implications for Leadership Training in the Military. *Defence Horizon Journal*; Sapolsky, R. M. (2017). Behave! The biology of humans at our best and worst. In *Penguin Press* (1st ed.). https://doi.org/10.1111/1467-8357.00356; Waller, J. (2002). *Becoming Evil: How Ordinary People Commit Genocide and Mass Killing*. https://doi.org/10.1001/jama.300.6.737.

for enrollment in selection procedures. After all, failure to cooperate can risk one's career, income or position within the military hierarchy. As a result, we should expect less motivation amongst young people to join the military, and for military professionals to stay, which may have severe consequences for a military's readiness. Moreover, because of these added limitations on the individual's privacy, at least concerning physical, mental health and character disposition, even those who do opt to stay in the military will feel less secure, which may negatively affect well-being and job satisfaction.

2 Physiological Feedback as a Measure of Excellence; Implications for the Individual

In an ideal world, from the perspective of selection procedures, privacy would not play a role and screening procedures would only be restrained by technological and intellectual limitations. In such a scenario, selection procedures could freely collect and utilise physiological and psychological feedback data to ensure that prospective recruits, as well as candidates for specific positions, meet whatever standards have been set in advance. Moreover, with the advance in scientific discovery, these standards could be updated continuously. As such, models would become increasingly effective at identifying excellent candidates while leaving room to adjust standards such, that enough individuals make it through to fulfil all required positions.

However, perfect predictability would ultimately remain out of reach because of the interconnectedness and nonlinearity of biological systems. As such, a model based on probability, rather than certainty, would likely need to be adopted. In practice, this would, either implicitly or explicitly, lead to a Bayesian-style statistical model which incorporates vulnerability factors, present indicators of sub-optimal coping, and markers of excellence, and which can be updated as new information about both the markers under investigation and the individuals tested for them are coming available. If we take susceptibility to post-combat PTSD as an example, a predictive model would take on the following structure:

$$P(A \mid B) = \frac{\mathrm{p}(\mathrm{B}|\mathrm{A}).P(A)}{P(B|A).P(A) + P(B|A)\cdot P(not\ A)}$$

In which A represents the probability of getting PTSD, B the possibility of having had a traumatising combat experience, A|B the probability of having PTSD given that one had a traumatising combat experience and B|A the probability of having had a traumatising combat experience if one has PTSD.

The prevalence of post-combat PTSD amongst military personnel and veterans, e.i. p(A), currently ranges from 11 to 27 per cent depending on the presence of traumatic brain injury.[25] For the current thought experiment, we will use the prevalence reported by Fulton et al. in their 2015 meta-analysis of 33 studies; 23 per cent. Moreover, given that combat can be generally assumed to be a traumatising experience for most people, p(B) will approximate 1. Some individuals, however, it must be noted, remain relatively unfazed by the horrors of combat. This may result from a pathological lack of empathy, which has been associated with the dark triad traits (psychopathy, Machiavellianism and narcissism),[26] but may equally be the result of heightened levels of in-group commitment, especially when the in-group is under threat. Several studies indicate a role for oxytocin in both resilience against PTSD[27] and elevated in-group commitment/ethnocentrism.[28] Likewise, the neuropeptide β-endorphin has been associated with both social belonging[29] and resilience against

25 Alexandra Loignon, Marie Christine Ouellet and Geneviève Belleville, 'A Systematic Review and Meta-Analysis on PTSD Following TBI among Military/Veteran and Civilian Populations' (2020) 35 Journal of Head Trauma Rehabilitation E21; Jessica J Fulton and others, 'The Prevalence of Posttraumatic Stress Disorder in Operation Enduring Freedom/ Operation Iraqi Freedom (OEF/OIF) Veterans: A Meta-Analysis' (2015) 31 Journal of Anxiety Disorders 98.

26 Julie Blais and Scott Pruysers, 'The Power of the Dark Side: Personality, the Dark Triad, and Political Ambition' (2017) 113 Personality and Individual Differences 167; Nadja Heym and others, 'Empathy at the Heart of Darkness: Empathy Deficits That Bind the Dark Triad and Those That Mediate Indirect Relational Aggression' (2019) 10 Frontiers in Psychiatry 1; Phillip S Kavanagh, Tania D Signal and Nik Taylor, 'The Dark Triad and Animal Cruelty: Dark Personalities, Dark Attitudes, and Dark Behaviors' (2013) 55 Personality and Individual Differences 666.

27 Laura Nawijn and others, 'Intranasal Oxytocin Increases Neural Responses to Social Reward in Post-Traumatic Stress Disorder' 212; Jenni Leppanen and others, 'Meta-Analysis of the Effects of Intranasal Oxytocin on Interpretation and Expression of Emotions' (2017) 78 Neuroscience and Biobehavioral Reviews 125 >.

28 (de Dreu et al. 2012; De Dreu et al. 2011; De Dreu et al. 2010)

29 Bronwyn Tarr and others, 'Synchrony and Exertion during Dance Independently Raise Pain Threshold and Encourage Social Bonding' (2015) 11 Biology Letters 0; Sandra Manninen and others, 'Social Laughter Triggers Endogenous Opioid Release in Humans.' (2017) 37 The Journal of neuroscience: the official journal of the Society for Neuroscience 6125; Katerina VA Johnson and Robin IM Dunbar, 'Pain Tolerance Predicts Human Social Network Size' (2016) 6 Scientific Reports 1; Martin Lang and others, 'Sync

PTSD,[30] although contrary to oxytocin, β-endorphin seems to stimulate passive coping strategies. As such, given that the prevalence of dark triad traits in the general population amounts to approximately 2 per cent, and it can be assumed that a minority of the individuals involved in combat naturally have a psychological constitution that allows for lethal out-group violence, p(B) will approximate, but probably never reach 1.

Moreover, because the probability of having had a traumatising experience is a prerequisite for a PTSD diagnosis,[31] and that the vast majority of post-mission PTSD cases do result from combat experiences, p(B|A) will approximate 1.[32] However, some cases will involve individuals who have been traumatised by other, non-combat related, events such as accidents, sexual assault or participation in, or witnessing of, extreme violence outside of the context of combat (i.e. unlawful executions, gang rape, genocide, etc.). In fact, the prevalence of PTSD in military personnel who engaged in extreme acts of unlawful violence is significantly higher than that of those who merely witnessed combat or even actively partaken in it.[33] If we assume, for this thought experiment that around 5 per cent[34] of the post-mission PTSD cases is not directly combat-related, the model, prior to the input of vulnerability factors and markers of excellence looks like this:

to Link: Endorphin-Mediated Synchrony Effects on Cooperation' (2017) 127 Biological Psychology 191.

30 Mac Gillavry and Ullrich (n 10); Ullrich and Mac Gillavry (n 8); Danka Savic and others, 'Posttraumatic and Depressive Symptoms in β-Endorphin Dynamics' (2015) 181 Journal of Affective Disorders 61; Troy Lisa Holbrook and others, 'Morphine Use after Combat Injury in Iraq and Post-Traumatic Stress Disorder' (2010) 362 The new england journal of medicine 110.

31 American Psychiatric Association, *Diagnostic and Statistical Manual of Mental Disorders* (*5th* (2013); World Health Organization, 'The ICD-10 Classification of Mental and Behavioural Disorders: Diagnostic Criteria for Research' (1993) 155.

32 Note here, that a PTSD diagnosis presupposes previous traumatic experience, having been traumatised does not nessesarily lead to a PTSD diagnosis.

33 Chen Xue and others, 'A Meta-Analysis of Risk Factors for Combat-Related PTSD among Military Personnel and Veterans' (2015) 10 PLoS ONE 1; Barbara L Pitts and others, 'Killing versus Witnessing Trauma: Implications for the Development of PTSD in Combat Medics' (2014) 25 Military Psychology 537; Michael Koenigs and Jordan Grafman, 'Posttraumatic Stress Disorder: The Role of Medial Prefrontal Cortex and Amygdala' (2009) 15 Neuroscientist 540.

34 This number might drop significantly if a similar model is applied to moral fortutide because many non-combat related cases are the result of severe breaches of ethical boundaries by in-group members. As such, it makes sense to focus this analysis on combat related PTSD only.

$$p(PTSD\ diagnosis \mid traumatised) = \frac{\text{p(traumatised} \mid PTSD\ diagnosis)\cdot p\left(PTSD\ diagnosis\right)}{\text{(traumatised} \mid PTSD\ diagnosis)\cdot p\left(PTSD\ diagnosis\right) + \text{p(traumatised} \mid PTSD\ diagnosis)\cdot p\left(no\ PTSD\ diagnosis\right)}$$

Or:

$$P(PTSD\,diagnosis \mid traumatised) = \frac{.95\cdot.23}{.95\cdot.23+.95\cdot.77} = .230$$

However, screening and selection procedures enable the specification of both vulnerability factors and markers of heightened resilience, which changes the prior p(A) = the prevalence of PTSD in a military population, to the prevalence of PTSD in a military population which portrays or does not portray certain characteristics. In effect p(A) would represent ∑p(effect sizes of vulnerability factors) – ∑p(effect sizes of markers of resilience. This would lead to a model which can both be updated and for which a cut-off rate can be established;

$$p(PTSD\ diagnosis \mid traumatised) = \frac{\text{p(traumatised} \mid PTSD\,diagnosis)\cdot p\left(\Sigma^{p}\left(\begin{matrix}\text{effect sizes of}\\ \text{vulnerability factors}\end{matrix}\right) - \Sigma^{p}\left(\begin{matrix}\text{effect sizes of}\\ \text{markers of resilience}\end{matrix}\right)\right)}{\text{(traumatised} \mid PTSD\,diagnosis)\cdot p\left(PTSD\,diagnosis\right) + \text{p(traumatised} \mid PTSD\ diagnosis)\cdot p\left(no\,PTSD\,diagnosis\right)}$$

It is in this equation, that the ethical issue concerning privacy presents itself most clearly; to root out individuals for whom p(A|B) exceeds a predetermined threshold, exceeding amounts of tests into the core of one's being need to be performed to individualise p(A).

Moreover, many of the physiological systems required to specify an increasingly individualised p(A) have a wider effect on behaviour and well-being than just vulnerability to post-combat PTSD. There are for instance indications that, in a subset of patients with PTSD, dopamine signaling to the cortical regions of the brain may be disrupted or that dopamine receptor function in these regions may be suboptimal.[35] Similar issues have, however, been reported for several attention-related disorders including attention-deficit/hyperactive disorder (ADHD), attention deficit disorder (ADD) and restless leg syndrome.[36] Unsurprisingly, there is a relatively high comorbidity between PTSD and ADHD,[37] while methylphenidate, a common neurotropic medication for ADHD, alleviates symptoms in a subpopulation of PTSD patients.[38] Similarly, a common genetic variation on the μ-opioid receptor gene appears to provide the carrier with a certain level of protection from PTSD but might also enhance dopamine signalling to the nucleus accumbens (a core component of the reward network), which may predispose the carrier to binge drinking.[39] In addition, an over-active opioid system has been associated with autism,[40] while the μ-opioid receptor antagonist, naltrexone, has been shown to simulate social behaviours in a subpopulation of children with autism.[41] As such, any system which may be relevant for incorporation in p(A) may carry a wealth of information about other aspects of the individual's being.

35 Jan Haaker and others, 'Single Dose of L-Dopa Makes Extinction Memories Context-Independent and Prevents the Return of Fear' (2013) 110 Proceedings of the National Academy of Sciences of the United States of America; BFP Broekman, M Olff and F Boer, 'The Genetic Background to PTSD' (2007) 31 Neuroscience and Biobehavioral Reviews 348; Jason C Lee, Lei Philip Wang and Joe Z Tsien, 'Dopamine Rebound-Excitation Theory: Putting Brakes on PTSD' (2016) 7 Frontiers in Psychiatry; Thomas McLaughlin and others, 'Putative Dopamine Agonist (KB220Z) Attenuates Lucid Nightmares in PTSD Patients: Role of Enhanced Brain Reward Functional Connectivity and Homeostasis Redeeming Joy' (2015) 4 Journal of Behavioral Addictions 106.

36 Alexandra J Richardson and others, 'Docosahexaenoic Acid for Reading, Cognition and Behavior in Children Aged 7–9 Years: A Randomized, Controlled Trial (The DOLAB Study)' (2012) 7 PLoS ONE 1; Tejas R Mehta and others, 'Neurobiology of ADHD: A Review' (2019) 6 Current Developmental Disorders Reports 235.

37 Kevin M Antshel and others, 'The Neuropsychological Profile of Comorbid Post-Traumatic Stress Disorder in Adult ADHD' (2016) 20 Journal of Attention Disorders 1047.

38 S Aga-Mizrachi and others, 'Methylphenidate and Desipramine Combined Treatment Improves PTSD Symptomatology in a Rat Model' (2014) 4 Translational Psychiatry.

39 Nicole R Nugent and others, 'OPRM1 and Diagnosis-Related Posttraumatic Stress Disorder in Binge-Drinking Patients Living with HIV' (2012) 16 AIDS and Behavior 2171.

40 Lucie P Pellissier and others, 'M Opioid Receptor, Social Behaviour and Autism Spectrum Disorder: Reward Matters' (2018) 175 British Journal of Pharmacology 2750; Jaak Panksepp, Najma Najam and Frieda Soares, 'Morphine Reduces Social Cohesion in Rats' (1979) 11 Pharmacology, Biochemistry and Behavior 131.

41 Barbara K Kolmen and others, 'Naltrexone in Young Autistic Children: A Double-Blind, Placebo-Controlled Crossover Study' (1995) 34 Journal of the American Academy of Child

3 Conclusion

In this paper, we call attention to the issue of privacy in the military in an age in which both political pressure and technological advancement call for increased research into, and screening for, both vulnerability factors of suboptimal coping and markers of excellence. The two main points we address here are "accidental data", i.e. data that is collected for context, but that does not itself form the focus of the research, and the interconnectedness of biological systems which leads, among other things, to a situation in which even relevant data, from a military perspective, can yield a wealth of information about an individual that does not directly pertain to the military but may nonetheless be of a highly sensitive nature. As such, this wealth of potentially available information about the individual, ranging from vulnerability factors for physical and mental health issues, predispositions towards certain types of behaviour, genetic data, etc. may constitute data, which they may not want to know about themselves and, moreover, may not want to be available to others.

In a civilian context, it would be a relatively straight-forward matter to set certain limitations on data collection to protect the individual's right to privacy. However, military professionals, especially those in combat positions, routinely find themselves in high-risk/high-stress environments for prolonged periods, which may have lasting negative consequences for the individual. Moreover, and more immediately pressing, frontline troops, while on mission, are equipped with the means to do serious harm to both themselves and others. Any unit of data, which can avoid lasting psychological damage or a situation in which one, willingly or by accident, inflicts harm on others outside of the rules of engagement, it may therefore be argued, is extremely relevant. Not collecting it could, itself, be viewed as a moral failure.

This juxtaposition between the needs of the military and the individual is further eventuated by recent dramatic changes in the nature warfare itself. As evidenced by the current conflict in Ukraine, even in confrontations between conventional forces, a relatively small but better equipped, trained and motivated force can hold out effectively against, what is at least on paper, one of the most powerful militaries in the world. Drones, hand-held anti-tank and air-defense missile systems, and guided rocket artillery systems and other 'smart' munitions, have drastically reshaped the battlefield. Such systems, however,

---

and Adolescent Psychiatry 223; Heidi M Feldman, Barbara K Kolmen and Alda Maria Gonzaga, 'Naltrexone and Communication Skills in Young Children with Autism' (1999) 38 Journal of the American Academy of Child and Adolescent Psychiatry 587.

require highly skilled troops to operate them, which increases the emphasis on selection and training procedures.

In an age where the public sentiment can turn easily and in which complex weapon-systems dominate the battlefield, data-collection on military personnel, for both scientific and recruitment purposes, is paramount in the strive for excellence. However, for all its promise, there are some serious ethical issues with data-collection. In this paper we aimed to raise some of these issues.

CHAPTER 7

Toxic Legacies: Right-Wing Extremism, Military Cultures, Perceptions of Betrayal and Military Ethics

Andrea Ellner

1 Introduction

The theme of this year's conference asked whether military ethics is keeping pace with the changing character of warfare. This paper is interested in the context within which this question is navigated. Two observations on three decades of liberal interventions triggered the analysis. One, in declared policy these interventions were built to a considerable degree on narratives around an ethics of care and (global) social justice,[1] as opposed to traditional concepts of national security, but they achieved hardly any of their aims. Two, the same decades have seen a significant increase in far and extreme right-wing or white supremacist activity which is particularly dangerous, because it is increasingly internationally networked and manifest not only across most civilian societies, but also the military and parts of the political structures, that is, political parties, of NATO countries.[2] The ideology of such groups clashes profoundly with ethics of care and social justice. It privileges purity and loyalty to the nation, which is constructed as white, and heightens gender power hierarchies and stereotypes. Historical precedent suggests that some service members and veterans who feel betrayed will swell their ranks, seeking solace in their communities and ideology.

These developments pose profound challenges to existing liberal democratic models of civil-military relations, to military transformation towards a more diverse and inclusive culture, which is in part adaptation to recruitment

1 See for example Barnett Rubin 'Afghanistan and Threats to Human Security' *Social Science Research Council items* (Social Science Research Council, 1 November 2001) <https://items.ssrc.org/after-september-11/afghanistan-and-threats-to-human-security/>.

2 Daniel Koehler 'Right-Wing Extremism and Terrorism in Europe Current Developments and Issues for the Future' (2016) 6 *PRISM* (2016) 2, 85–104 <https://cco.ndu.edu/PRISM/PRISM-Volume-6-no-2/Article/839011/right-wing-extremism-and-terrorism-in-europe-current-developments-and-issues-fo/>.

 | DOI:10.1163/9789004544314_009

requirements and the changing operational environment, and to the preparedness of armed forces for the conduct of operations. From here emerge in turn the profound challenges for military ethics, whose conceptual advancement and application in the NATO context over the past three decades has relied on assumptions that are rooted in liberal norms or at least declared aspirations to meet these norms. The far or extreme right and white supremacists feel threatened by these norms and their manifestations and respond with uncompromising contestation or even violent rejection.

The numbers of problematic individuals may be small compared to the overall size of armed forces, but the salient criterion for measuring risk is not quantitative, but qualitative impact. Acts of extreme non-state violence have historically been planned, prepared and perpetrated by relatively small numbers of people, though often with wider active or tacit support. Key to their success is to have the right people with the right skills in the right place to bring together the necessary supplies and will to act. Right-wing violent extremist are targeting members of, or seeking to join, the armed forces in order to have access to either such supplies or military training. Each individual thus equipped can exponentially increase the capacity for violence of a civilian or paramilitary group. Some have had support or cover from the wider security services, but examining this goes beyond the scope of the current analysis.

In preventing further deterioration of the situation, this analysis argues, military ethicists have a role to play in advising on policy development as well as designing and delivering professional military education, which needs to address all ranks from the private to the general officer in the senior leadership team. In order to be able to play these roles effectively we must understand the problems, their causes and their manifestations better. Subsequently, military ethics needs to reflect on its underlying assumptions and adapt not only how it defines its purpose, but also what military ethicists do in order to contribute to pushing back or even reversing the influence of far-right extremism.

This analysis takes the first step. It seeks to build up a picture of the nature of the problem and begin to identify where and why military ethics needs to reflect on its own underlying assumptions and develop responses to these challenges. Without that, military ethics risks failing to keep pace with profound threats to its essentially liberal foundations and raison d'être: the regulation of the use of force to minimise harms and aid in facilitating better peace.

The paper begins by charting the empirical context and rationale of the analysis. It then briefly introduces and critically examines a typology of problem areas related to links between right-wing extremists or white supremacists and the military. The section highlights the need to be able to explore and explain the dynamics of the wider context as well as phenomena that cut across the four categories of the model. The subsequent two sections examine cases of right-wing extremists in armed forces, and their relevance to diversity and inclusion within the military. These are followed by a comparison of official responses to the problems in selected countries, and reflections on how military ethicists should and can conduct further research on, engage with and address these challenges in the development of concepts, policy input, and professional military education (PME) and training.

2 A Toxic Brew

For several years now concerns have re-emerged amongst members of governments, parliaments, military leaders and scholars in various NATO countries about the extreme right, sometimes better described as white supremacists, again expanding links between their civilian networks and members of the military. In the wake of the withdrawal of intervention forces from Afghanistan in 2021 political and military leaders and analysts in North American and many European NATO countries feared that such groups could draw further on a sense of having been betrayed by politicians and the military leadership amongst some of the soldiers and veterans who had been deployed to Iraq and Afghanistan, and indeed there was early evidence of this occurring amongst veterans.[3]

The prospect is seriously disconcerting considering that large numbers of serving members of the US armed forces and veterans took part in the storming of the Capitol building in Washington, DC, on 6 January 2021. These events were on the one hand contingent on the US socio-political and economic situation; there are credible witness testimonies today of outgoing President Donald Trump playing a pivotal role in rousing not just his peaceful supporters, but also those from the far right and white supremacist spectrum, who he knew were armed, into action.[4] Yet, the influence of the far or even extreme right in formal politics and structures of government is not unique to the US, as Jason Stanley has shown persuasively in his detailed study of the rise, methods and increasing power of the far and extreme right in governments and societies across the globe.[5]

3 Annelies Pauwels, 'Afghan withdrawal may spark ex-forces terrorism in Europe' *EU Observer* (Brussels, 28 September 2021) <https://euobserver.com/opinion/152958>.

4 Sam Cabral, 'January 6 hearings: Trump urged armed supporters to storm Capitol – aide' *BBC News* (London, 29 June 2020) <https://www.bbc.co.uk/news/world-us-canada-61971428>.

5 Jason Stanley, *How Fascism Works – The Politics of US and THEM* (Random House 2018).

Whilst Stanley does not specifically discuss their influence in and on the armed forces, he demonstrates that this is a serious threat to liberal democracies. That threat is the background for this analysis, because by extension it also challenges extant models of civil-military relations in liberal democracies. Although they are historically and socio-culturally contingent, they are all based on the principle of the monopoly of the state on force and acknowledge the supreme authority of the elected government over the armed forces. Those that endorse the relevance of military ethics do so with an understanding that it shares the liberal roots of international law and the law of armed conflict or international humanitarian law. Right-wing extremists and white supremacists reject the underlying rationale of not only liberal democracy, but also such cosmopolitan perspectives.

This rejection became amplified over the wars in Iraq and especially in Afghanistan, as an investigation of social media by *Politico* in the wake of the withdrawal from Afghanistan demonstrated. It found that on Twitter "far-right supporters associated the Islamic militants with the Confederate States of America, the pro-slavery side in the US Civil War. Others made direct comparisons between the Taliban and the US founding fathers. And under the tagline "one struggle," another highlighted how both the far-right and the Taliban shared a common purpose against liberal values."[6]

In 2021 Raffaello Pantucci and Kyler Ong found that the growth of extreme right-wing groups and violence was stalling, but extreme right-wing influences in armed forces were growing more dangerous. They noted in particular the sentencing of extreme right, white supremacists for their parts in the 6 January 2021 events in Washington, DC. They record that a German Special Forces unit and a military honour guard were disbanded for their extreme right-wing associations. In France purportedly serving and semi-retired service personnel with extreme right-wing convictions warned in an open letter of a civil war sparked by the government's "concessions" to Islamism; "a former local politician and far-right conspiracy theorist (…) was also charged, amongst other terrorist acts, for plotting a coup against the government and recruiting soldiers to facilitate the act".[7]

6 Mark Scott 'Western far-right groups claim Taliban victory as their own' *POLITICO* (Arlington, VA, 18 August 2021) https://www.politico.eu/article/far-right-taliban-afghanistan-social-media-facebook-twitter/.

7 Raffaelo Pantucci and Kyler Ong, 'Extreme Right Violence in the West: In Remission?' (2022) 14 *Counter-Terrorist Trends and Analyses* (2022) 1 <https://raffaellopantucci.com/tag/far-right/>.

The growing sense of threats to the constitutional foundations and the functioning of liberal democracy have been playing out most publicly around the congressional inquiry into the storming of the Capitol in Washington, DC.[8] In part because of public pressure from media and parliamentarians, the German government, Bundeswehr and intelligence services have also been facing up to the problem.[9] In Britain, the House of Commons Select Committee on Intelligence and Security reported in July 2022 on its inquiry into the extreme right, including in the security services.[10] MI5, the domestic intelligence service, publicly reinforced the Committee's call for enhanced funding to address the "growing threat" of right-wing extremism.[11]

Tackling these threats demands effective constitutional governance, but they are a profoundly political problem. Where it involves the military, there is a need for engagement in critical discourses within the armed forces, and between them and on the one hand government and on the other hand civilian society. It is not a new phenomenon. Links between the far right and the military have waxed and waned over time, but they have a long history in countries such as Britain,[12] Germany,[13] and the US.[14] Yet, today the far or even extreme right has either established itself in formal politics or is exerting strong influence

8 David Smith, 'January 6 testimony tells chilling tale of democracy hanging by a thread' *The Guardian* (Manchester, 12 July 2022) < https://www.theguardian.com/us-news/2022/jul/12/january-6-hearing-trump-analysis>.

9 „'Aktionsplan Rechtsextremismus': Innenministerin Nancy Faeser mit den Chefs der Inlandsgeheimdienste". *Phoenix von ARD and ZDF*. 15 March 2022. https://www.youtube.com/watch?v=uUINFCsCDkk.

10 Intelligence and Security Committee of Parliament (2022) *Extreme Right-Wing Terrorism* HC459 (London: HH Associates 2020) <https://isc.independent.gov.uk/wp-content/uploads/2022/07/E02710035-HCP-Extreme-Right-Wing-Terrorism_Accessible.pdf>.

11 John Paul Rathbone Rathbone, John Paul, 'MI5 needs more funds to combat rightwing terrorism in UK, say MPs' *Financial Times* (London, 13 July 2022) <https://www.ft.com/content/e52cbb92-7488-4294-b65d-ec999c18079c>.

12 Daniel Jones, 'The Far Right Has a History of Infiltrating the British Army' *Fair Observer* (Belmont, CA, 21 March, 2019) <https://www.fairobserver.com/region/europe/uk-far-right-british-army-extremism-europe-news-17712/>.

13 Lucius Teidelbaum, „Ein besonders sensibler Bereich"' – Meinung: Rechtsextremismus in der Bundeswehr' *Bundeszentrale für Politische Bildung* (Berlin, 1 April 2018) <https://www.bpb.de/themen/rechtsextremismus/dossier-rechtsextremismus/274176/ein-besonders-sensibler-bereich/>; Volker Wagener, 'The Bundeswehr's image problem – is it overrun with right-wing extremists?' *Deutsche Welle* (Berlin, 3 May 2017) <https://www.dw.com/en/the-bundeswehrs-image-problem-is-it-overrun-with-right-wing-extremists/a-38684538>.

14 Kathleen Belew, *Bring the War Home – The White Power Movement and Paramilitary America* (Harvard University Press 2018).

on mainstream party politics in several NATO countries. Extreme-right, white supremacist and hate groups, such as the US-founded 'Atomwaffendivision', are also very well connected internationally both vertically above and underground, and horizontally, across borders and continents.[15] Hence the picture is highly complex, fragmented and multidimensional.

3 An Emerging Conceptual Framework

Research into the influence and prevalence of the extreme right within or its connections with national armed forces of NATO countries has received more attention over the past few years. Yet, efforts at conceptualisation are still young. In 2022 a team of authors at the International Centre for Counter-Terrorism (ICCT) created a model typology.[16] Through a meta-analysis of existing literature on military-related right-wing extremism in twelve NATO countries, inter alia the US, Canada, Germany, the UK, France and the Netherlands, they arrived at four "problem areas":

1: Right-wing extremist violence perpetrated by military personnel
2: Right-wing extremist violence facilitated by military personnel
3: Ideologically motivated hate crimes or violation of procedures and rules of engagement while on deployment
4: Activities and behaviours that hamper diversity and inclusion efforts

This typology is a first step towards a more systematic approach to studying this phenomenon, but closer consideration raises questions about the underlying logic. There is an inherent conceptual incompatibility between the first pairing and the second two. The first pairing categorises how service members might be directly or indirectly implicated in perpetrating extremist violence; that this is of interest to a think tank that studies terrorism is self-evident. The problem is that empirical evidence cannot necessarily be neatly divided between the two categories, because networks can be complex and their members may have different roles ranging from supply to violent action or both.

15 Alexander Epp; Roman Höfner, ‚Das Hass-Netzwerk „Atomwaffendivision"' *Der Spiegel* (Hamburg, 24 August 2018) <https://www.spiegel.de/politik/das-hass-netzwerk-atomwaffen-division-a-61ff2ccc-0002-0001-0000-000159073499>; ‚Atomwaffen Division' *Southern Poverty Law Center* (Montgomery, AL, undated) https://www.splcenter.org/fighting-hate/extremist-files/group/atomwaffen-division.

16 Teun van Dongen et al, *Right-Wing Extremism in the Military Right-Wing Extremism in the Military – A Typology of the Threat* (International Centre for Counter-Terrorism, May 2022) <https://icct.nl/app/uploads/2022/05/Right-wing-extremism-in-the-military-1.pdf>.

For example, several cases that have come to light in Germany over the past few years combined plans to take direct action with the supply of materials which might be regarded as aiding and abetting terrorist attacks. The 'Nordkreuz' network of civilians, members of the police and the military for example was a group of 'preppers', supplying and collecting ammunition or explosives in anticipation of a Day X, when a civil war would begin and the collapse of state authority in Germany would make self-defence essential, but they were also planning attacks on politicians.[17] Members of the groups thus had roles that were spread across the spectrum of supply and action. It would be difficult to categorise those who covered both ends of the spectrum or the group as a whole under either problem area one or two.

The second pair of problem areas is not naturally related to the first two. They deal with the impact of extreme right-wing groups on the military as an organisation with regard to both the exercise of its essential external function, the conduct of military operations on behalf of the state, and the internal development of its organisational culture.

From an ethical and a political perspective internal culture and external conduct are linked. Beginning with the political dimension and focusing on civil-military relations, scholars such as Morris Janowitz have argued that a military population whose demographic profile reflects society and whose members share the fundamental values of civilian society, even if their civil liberties are more limited due to the nature of their profession, is more likely to perceive itself as connected to that society and prepared to risk limb and life or kill in war on behalf of that society. This matters therefore to both aspects of civil-military relations. One, the relationship between the military and society from whom the former also draws its personnel and material resources and two that between military and government which in liberal democracies is the constitutionally entitled authority to order the use of force for political ends.

Through the lens of ethics, organisational culture or command climate, a link between external conduct and internal organisation can be illustrated on the example of ethical conduct of service members. If service-people practice in their daily professional life by acting in accordance with their service's virtues, military ethos and ethics that are grounded in the liberal democratic tradition and its socio-cultural manifestations today, they can be expected to behave accordingly on operations. If they do not live by these values and virtues in their daily professional life, they neither acquire a routine nor the

17 Florian Flade, 'The Insider Threat: Far-Right Extremism in the German Military and Police' (2021) 14 *CTC Sentinel* (2021) 5, 3 <https://ctc.usma.edu/the-insider-threat-far-right-extremism-in-the-german-military-and-police/>.

necessary consciousness before they deploy. It is then unlikely that they can make ethical decisions and act accordingly under the pressure of combat or even combat support in major armed conflict or in stabilisation or peacekeeping operations which demand ethical sensitivity in the many tasks involving close work with local civilians, armed forces or allies.

The four problem areas are implicitly related to such processes and linkages, but they do not specifically pull them in or naturally invite their analysis. They are rather more focused on the actions and behaviours of extreme right-wing proponents and less accommodating of causalities and correlations or even the qualities of the ideology, the kinds of values extreme right-wing actors reject, and their motivations. For military ethicists these are central issue areas. The ICCT typology is thus a useful tool for categorising the types of problematic effects right-wing extremists can have inside or in association with the military. It is of more limited use for identifying and understanding why and how the extreme right is able to acquire such capacity and positions. For this we need to explore dynamics that cut across the four problem areas, as the following two sections will begin to do.

4 Military Personnel Implicated in or Associated with Right-Wing Extremist Violence

The ICCT study found a steep increase within the past three or so years of military personnel themselves committing violent acts. The most significant rise was documented by Seth G. Jones of the Center for Strategic and International Studies (CSIS) for the US, where right-wing extremist active duty and reserve personnel committed no domestic terrorist attacks in 2018, 1.5 percent in 2019 and 6.4 percent in 2020.[18] Military personnel's and veterans' involvement in the storming of the Capitol weighed heavily. There were individual partially or fully prevented incidents in Canada, where Corey Hurren crashed into the Prime Ministerial compound and attempted to arrest Prime Minister Trudeau, and in Germany, where Franco A., a Lieutenant in the Bundeswehr, was arrested for planning a terrorist attack under the guise of being a Syrian refugee.

For military ethicists this case will be an interesting study, because he had attended the French military academy Saint-Cyr in 2013. Concerned about suspect thinking informing his dissertation, French staff at Saint-Cyr raised the

18 S.G. Jones et al., *The Military, Police, and the Rise of Terrorism in the United States* (*Washington, DC, Center for Strategic and International Studies, 2021*) <*https://www.csis.org/analysis/military-police-and-rise-terrorism-united-states*> cited in van Dongen (n16), 4.

alarm with their German colleagues; after interviewing him the latter found his conduct unproblematic. Yet, in 2022 he was convicted of planning a major attack intended to harm Germany's security and sentenced to five years and six months in prison.[19] There are clearly lessons to be learnt.

These specific cases have to be seen within a bigger picture though. Further comparative research is likely to show that some of the historical trajectories and current dynamics of the involvement of extreme-right or white supremacist groups with the armed forces will be country-specific, but some common framework conditions are already emerging. These include individual responses to deployments in Iraq and Afghanistan as well as the response to the withdrawal from Afghanistan in August 2021 and its aftermath. They fit into a historical pattern.

In *Bring the War Home* Kathleen Belew traces in considerable detail the waxing and waning of white supremacist movements from the foundation of the KKK to the Oklahoma Bombing in 1995.[20] Relatively few veterans joined extreme right or white supremacist movements. They were motivated by a confluence of several factors. A sense of betrayal by their government and civilian society combined with difficulties in finding economic security and alienation due to societal liberalisation. After the Vietnam War they no longer recognised US society's values which the civil rights movement has changed. Unable to adapt their values to this societal change, the only choice they saw was to try to save society from itself and recover 'traditional' white values, but in order to have the desired impact they felt they needed to bring the war home.

This notion of bringing the war home recurs today in and outside the US. For example, the German Society of Reservists distanced itself immediately after a grouping emerged on social media in mid-April 2021 which described itself as *Veteranen-Pool* (Veterans' Pool). It was seeking to recruit soldiers, veterans and reservists "offensively", reminding them of their "Soldierly conscience" („soldatisches Bewusstsein") and of their oath of service. *Veteranen-Pool*'s aim is described as enticing individuals with links to the Bundeswehr to participate in "disruptive actions" (Störaktionen) against the state, that is, not peaceful demonstrations but "deliberate provocations of the state". They openly declared that they considered themselves to be in a "state of war".[21]

---

19 Raquel Erdtmann, ‚Die gefährlichen Gedanken des Franco A.' *Die Zeit* (Hamburg, 24 July 2022) <https://www.zeit.de/2022/30/bundeswehrsoldat-franco-a-prozess-anschlagsplaene/komplettansicht>.

20 Belew (n14).

21 Die Redaktion, 'Reservistenverband Distanziert sich von "Veteranen-Pool"' *die reserve* (Bonn, 29 April 2021) <https://www.reservistenverband.de/magazin-die-reserve/reservistenverband-distanziert-sich-von-veteranen-pool/>.

The Chairman of the Federation of German Operations Veterans (Bund Deutscher Einsatzveteranen), Bernhard Drescher, saw increasing support for organisations such as *Veteranen Pool* or *Veteranen 5 nach 12* (Veterans 5 (minutes) past Midnight) as a direct result of veterans' perception that the concerns of soldiers and veterans had "never mattered". He emphasised that the veterans' feeling of senselessness and betrayal of the mission, of Afghans and of Bundeswehr soldiers risked "emotionally losing a group of people who are important to the state".[22] The problem goes beyond *the* state, though.

In December 2021 the Canadian National Security and Intelligence Review Agency (NSIRA) warned of the well documented existence of white supremacists in the defence force, but this included also reservists and has international impact. According to Amanda Connelly

"'White supremacist groups actively seek individuals with prior military training and experience, or conversely, encourage individuals to enlist in order to gain access to specialized training, tactics and equipment' the NSIRA report determined. The most recent high-profile example was Patrik Mathews, an ex-reservist, who was recently sentenced to nine years in prison for his role in a violent plot to provoke a race war in Virginia. Mathews was a member of The Base, a militant white supremacist organization, who fled his Manitoba home to link up with the group's members in the US."[23]

The internationalisation of right-wing and white supremacist networks and their effects is emerging as a key determinant for an urgent need to align risk assessments across NATO allies towards a common understanding of the threat in its various manifestations and the development of best practice in devising countermeasures as well as delivering preventative programmes within armed forces. Before we explore this, a closer look at the problem from a gender perspective will offer more nuanced insights into its impact on the armed forces.

---

22 ‚Bundeswehr in Afghanistan – Sorge vor Radikalisierung von Veteranen' *Tagesschau* (Hamburg, 25 August 2021) <https://www.tagesschau.de/inland/innenpolitik/afghanistan-veteranen-101.html>.

23 Amanda Connolly, 'Widespread systemic racism in Canadian military 'repulsing' new recruits: report' *Global News* (Vancouver, BC, 25 April 2022) <https://globalnews.ca/news/8784238/canadian-forces-systemic-racism-repulsing-new-recruits/>.

5 Gender Perspectives on Right-Wing Extremism in Armed Forces (and Society)

All NATO members are at least indirectly bound to gender integration and gender mainstreaming, that is, applying gender perspectives to the all aspects of the organisation. NATO has repeatedly committed itself to implementing the Women, Peace & Security Agenda.[24] Since its inception in 2000 the Agenda has evolved from a focus on women to gender and the role of gendered power hierarchies in societies' conflict-risk. NATO's commitment to the Agenda includes applying gender perspectives to all aspects of planning and conducting military operations. This external purpose is intended to be complemented by internal adaptation of organisational cultures, structures and processes so a more diverse population can thrive in a truly inclusive climate. NATO sees a clear linkage between the internal and external application and practice of normative policies and ethical behaviours.

Especially North European and American members have officially pursued such cultural transformation for years, even if implementation has been slow, and supported WPS policies at NATO level. Many Central and some Southern European members are more reluctant to engage; some prohibit gender studies at civilian universities.[25] Ideology of the far or extreme right plays into and gains succour from this and threatens the transformation of military cultures. Not all variants of extreme right-wing ideology valorise hyper-masculine images and behaviour, neither are women always see as passive or their agency limited to motherhood and caring. Recent research is demonstrating that women's roles in white supremacy or extreme right-wing groups are varied and often influential.[26] Men who venerate militarised hyper-masculinity and are thus attracted to the armed forces, however, do stereotype women in roles which are incompatible with women as combatants of equal standing to male soldiers.[27]

---

24 NATO, *Women, Peace and Security* (22 July 2022) https://www.nato.int/cps/en/natohq/topics_91091.htm.

25 Becky Prager, 'The Hungarian Ban in Gender Studies and its Implications for Democratic Freedom' *Harvard Journal of Law U& Gender* (2019) < https://harvardjlg.com/2019/01/the-hungarian-ban-on-gender-studies-and-its-implications-for-democratic-freedom/>.

26 Miranda Christou, 'The Fragile, Toxic Masculinity of White Supremacy' *RANTT* (New York, 18 September 2019) <https://rantt.com/the-fragile-toxic-masculinity-of-white-supremacy>.

27 Kathleen Blee, 'Where Do We Go from Here? Positioning Gender in Studies of the Far Right' (2020) 21 *Politics, Religion & Ideology* (2020) 4, 419f.

There is little research on correlations between sexual assault or misogynistic behaviour within military organisations and extreme right-wing views of service personnel. Hence we do not yet have a detailed understanding whether the presence of the latter is linked to a higher rate or greater severity of such incidents in military units. A 2020 study by the UN Security Council Counter-Terrorism Committee (CTED), however, highlighted the pivotal role of gender in extreme right-wing thinking, behaviour, power hierarchies and separation of spaces. Nationalist narratives around women as housewives and bearers of children whose supreme responsibility it is to guarantee "the survival of the nation" are merged with "anti-immigrant conspiracy theories such as 'the great replacement'" and this rhetoric "is frequently accompanied by violence against women (including incitement of rape) and marked by synergies between misogyny, violent right-wing extremism and terrorism (…) [allowing] more obscure misogynist groups – such as incels (involuntary celibates) – to act as a bridge to violent extreme-right wing groups and individuals."[28]

The study emphasises the importance of violent masculine identities as a complement to this framing of women's roles. Violence is considered a necessary response to white men's anxieties about their loss of power in an "ever-changing, multicultural landscape" and propaganda strategies and messages target men who are expected to be sympathetic to such fears of losing status. In 2018 the Anti-Defamation League demonstrated this fluidity between and mutual amplification of misogyny and racism in some detail, finding that "this cross-pollination means the largely anonymous outrage of the men's rights arena acts as a bridge to the white supremacist and anti-Semitic ideology of the alt right."[29]

Hence there is some evidence of a correlation or even causation between the two, but there is much room for further research, especially in military environments, because not many have asked some of the key questions as Eviane Leidig has argued. In her view, the study of terrorism associated with extreme right-wing groups or individuals, or men identifying as incels falls short, because it fails to recognise the normalisation of misogyny in patriarchal

---

28 UNSC Counter-Terrorism Committee, Executive Directorate, *Member States Concerned by the Growing and Increasingly Transnational Threat of Extreme Right-Wing Terrorism – CTED Trends Alert* (April 2020) <https://www.un.org/securitycouncil/ctc/sites/www.un.org.securitycouncil.ctc/files/files/documents/2021/Jan/cted_trends_alert_extreme_right-wing_terrorism.pdf>.

29 Anti-Defamation League, *When Women are the Enemy: The Intersection of Misogyny and White Supremacy* (New York, Center on Extremism 2018) <https://www.adl.org/sites/default/files/When%20Women%20are%20the%20Enemy%20-The%20Intersection%20of%20Misogyny%20and%20White%20Supremacy.pdf>.

societies, including in countries discussed here. She saw another context for amplification, because while "the phenomenon of incels (as well as far-right extremism) is fragmented, socially diverse, (…) perhaps most importantly, [it] amplifies mainstream gender norms that appear acceptable to the public."[30]

Military authorities and military ethicists need to recognise these blind spots, as this offers opportunities to address both patriarchal challenges of mainstream culture and the misogyny motivated by extreme right ideologies.

6 Ethics, Gender and Right-Wing Extremists in the Military

Although the process of culture change in the military is far from complete, there has been much progress in improving not only diversity but also inclusion in the North American and North European armed forces, as demonstrated for example by the opening up of virtually all roles to women and their rise into senior leadership positions. Some of this has been achieved through PME, but it has also been facilitated by research and policy analysis identifying barriers to greater equality and inclusion of women and other demographic minorities into the male dominated environment and culture of the armed forces. Military ethicists, who are seeking to promote ethical behaviour within armed forces, not least in order to promote its application on operations, continue to play a major role here.

PME is an obvious vehicle, but it needs to be led by a great deal more research on these issues. If we gain the ability to separate roots of misogynistic or other hateful behaviour in mainstream patriarchal thinking from right-wing extremism, we will be able to tailor PME much more effectively to countering the latter or identifying individuals of concern. This needs to be complemented by strengthening the moral courage of those who reject hateful or exclusionary thinking and are prepared to stand up for norms and values supporting diversity and inclusion.

In fact clearer recognition of links between misogyny and far or extreme right ideology may provide scope for identifying followers of the latter. For the daily interactions between service members and leaders, trainers or educators this may only offer indicators to flag up those who are relatively open about their hostility to the integration of women, ethnic minorities or LGBTQI+ people into the armed forces. Formal investigations of sexual harassment or

30 Eviane Leidig, 'Why Terrorism Studies Miss the Mark When It Comes To Incels' (International Centre for Counter-Terrorism, 31 August, 2021) <https://icct.nl/publication/why-terrorism-studies-miss-the-mark-when-it-comes-to-incels/>.

assault, bullying or racism, however, should also seek to identify causes of such behaviour with special attention to the possibility of extreme right-wing ideological motivations. Availability of these kinds of disaggregated data could be taken further to shed more light on extreme right-wing networks within the armed forces and potentially even their connections to civilian society.

An important caveat is in order here. This must not lead to the instrumentalization of DE&I education and training as an intelligence tool. The fundamental purpose of creating inclusive command and organisational cultures, processes and structures for western armed forces capable of addressing the manifold operational challenges in the emerging security environment must not be lost. Mills, Schmuhl and Capellan's exploration of the link between gender inequality or equality and male violence against women, not only but including from right-wing extremists, can point the way. They found that at state and regional levels as well as in occupational settings greater gender equality led to higher incidents of male violence against women, but in youth educational settings the correlation did not hold up. Here teaching and practicing greater gender equality reduced the levels of male violence against girls.[31] Replicating these results for adults in PME setting is not straightforward, but here too there is evidence that prolonged educational efforts on DE&I, including sexual assault prevention, can have a lasting effect.[32]

That and full recognition and inclusion of women's agency must remain the primary purpose of ethics and DE&I education in the military. Any counter-extremism benefits that might be gained in the process must be in support of this aim. Anything else would risk being unethical. Official responses to the challenges of right-wing extremism have so far neglected gender dimensions. Moreover, a broad comparison of approaches in four key NATO countries shows that there is considerable divergence and much scope for improvement, but there are also opportunities for military ethicists to engage meaningfully to a greater extent.

31 Mills, Colleen E., Margaret Schmuhl and Joel A. Capellan, 'Far-right violence as backlash against gender equality: A county-level analysis of structural and ideological gender inequality and homicides committed by far-right extremists' (2020) 43 *Journal of Crime and Justice* (2020) 5, 568–584.

32 Currier, Danielle M. and Jessica H. Carlson, 'Creating Attitudinal Change Through Teaching – How a Course on "Women and Violence" Changes Students' Attitudes About Violence Against Women' (2009) 24 *Journal of Interpersonal Violence* (2009) 10, 1735–1754.

7 Government Responses – Scope for Learning

In Germany, the scandal of the NSU (National Socialist Underground) enhanced the vigilance of the authorities. The NSU, a small group of right-wing extremists guilty of ten ideologically motivated murders, mostly of German citizens with a migrant background, bomb attacks and bank robberies between 1998 and 2011, remained undetected for years partly because of cover-ups and even assistance by individuals in the German security services; there were lingering suspicions of right-wing extremism being downplayed. One of its members, Uwe Mundlos, had brief military training. An initial parliamentary investigation of the NSU affair uncovered that until the late 1990s the Bundeswehr did not discharge conscripts even if the Bundesamt für den Militärischen Abschirmdienst (BAMAD), the federal intelligence service *inter alia* responsible for investigating unconstitutional activities in the Bundeswehr, had identified them.[33]

Concerns about surviving extreme right-wing ideology within the Bundeswehr have regularly attracted the attention of investigative journalists and some scholars since its foundation in 1955. With the intention of guarding against these risks the Bundeswehr adopted the concept of *Innere Führung* (inner leadership), a set of values grounded in foundational principles of liberal democracy. Intended as an internal moral compass for soldiers and the professional ethos of the military as an instrument of state, it seeks to promote the principle of individual responsibilities of and for good leadership and ethical behaviour within armed forces and their purpose, operations and conduct. It is based on the assumption that ethical leadership starts with the individual and governs good conduct of all others in the chain of command as well as the application of force within an ethical framework that seeks to protect human dignity.[34] This has not necessarily prevented problems, but it is a foundation on which military ethics can build scholarly work, policy development and PME.

The Bundeswehr has a dedicated Zentrum Innere Führung (Centre for Inner Leadership) and works closely with the Zentrum für ethische Bildung in den Streifkräften (*zebis*, Centre of Ethical Education in the Armed Forces). In 2020 the former published, with BAMAD, guidance on recognising right-wing

33 ‚Bundeswehr duldete bekennende Neonazis' *Die Zeit Online* (Hamburg, 8 November 2012) https://www.zeit.de/politik/deutschland/2012-11/nsu-bundeswehr-geheimdienst.

34 Markus Patenge, 'Innere Führung as an Attempt to Answer the Question of (Military) Force – Theological and Ethical Remarks on the Current Debate' (2021) *Ethics and Armed Forces* (2021) 2, 18–23 <http://www.ethikundmilitaer.de/fileadmin/ethics_and_armed_forces/Ethics-and-Armed-Forces-2021-2.pdf>.

extremism in language, symbols and in the publicity of political parties, such as the *Alternative für Deutschland* (AfD).[35] The BAMAD has a formal screening process for applicants to the Bundeswehr, but it is upon the latter to decide whether to reject them. Annual BAMAD reports, which are publicly presented to the Bundestag, now provide a growing database. Governments had already authorised active countermeasures and increased funding for the Federal Agency for Political Education which works inter alia with schools. In 2022 Minister for the Interior, Nancy Faeser, who is strongly committed to addressing right-wing extremism, presented an *Action Plan against Right-Wing Extremism* which includes engagement with the Bundeswehr.[36]

These activities are responses to evidence of extreme right-wing activity in the armed forces or connections of individual service members with like-minded networks in civilian society, and even a political party. For years the far right *Alternative für Deutschland* (AfD), which has seats in the Bundestag (Parliament), has focused on recruiting veterans and establishing itself as the political representative of Bundeswehr personnel and indeed its membership includes an exceptionally large number of veterans and retired senior officers; it must be noted that many Bundeswehr members object to its claims of speaking for them.[37] The party's compliance with the Constitution has long been called into question. In March 2020 the Federal Office for the Protection of the Constitution declared the so-called 'wing' (Der Flügel), a subsection of the AfD, a "verified right-wing extremist movement", the highest category of threat to the Constitution and its institutions. This led to the dissolution of the 'wing'. In March 2021 it classified the entire party as "case of concern" (Verdachtsfall). This means it can be put under enhanced observation by the internal security services for suspicion of unconstitutional activities, that is, right-wing extremism.[38]

There is a realisation that Germany, including the Bundeswehr, does have a serious problem that will need continued attention. If anything the problem is become more pressing in light of the mutual reinforcement of and by extreme

35 Zentrum Innere Führung and Bundesamt für den Militärischen Abschirmdienst, *Die Verteidigung unserer Werte: Gemeinsam gegen Extremismus* (Koblenz, 13 July 2020) <https://www.bundeswehr.de/de/organisation/weitere-bmvg-dienststellen/zentrum-innere-fuehrung/verteidigung-unserer-werte-275558>.

36 „Aktionsplan Rechtsextremismus"' (n9).

37 Maria Fiedler ,Truppen sammeln: Die AfD als Soldaten-Partei?' *Zentrum Liberale Moderne* (Berlin, 14 February 2020) <https://libmod.de/afd-bundeswehr-extremismus/>.

38 Christoph Kehlbach and Frank Bräutigam, ,AfD zum Verdachtsfall erklärt: Unter Beobachtung – was heißt das?' *Tagesschau* (Hamburg, 3 March 2021) <https://www.tagesschau.de/inland/innenpolitik/faq-afd-101.html>.

right-wing and white supremacist networks not only on an international scale, but also across 'causes'. In Britain evidence has been coming to light that so-called 'anti-vaxxer groups', who reject Covid-19 vaccinations on the basis of conspiracy narratives, are evolving into "US-style militias". They are reportedly actively affiliating with militia and white supremacists, including prominent players in the 6 January 2021 riots. Two UK-based groups, *Alpha Men Assemble* (AMA) and *Veterans 4 Freedom* have been targeting and successfully recruiting former members of the armed forces via social networks like Telegram.[39]

The conviction in 2018 of Cpl Mikko Vehvilainen for membership of *National Action*, a banned neo-Nazi terrorist group, galvanised the British Army's response. He has been working with three other soldiers who received different levels of punishment, and a recruiter within the Army. He had accumulated a sizeable weapons arsenal and Nazi paraphernalia.[40] All British armed forces recruits are vetted. In addition, since Vehvilainen's detection in 2017, military personnel identified as right-wing extremists have been referred to PREVENT, the British counter-terrorism programme, and the armed forces introduced

"unique prevention measures (e.g. mandatory training, cooperation with counterradicalization programs, guides for the detection of extremist ideology) that fit into the general logic of most CVE work, i.e. awareness of signs of concern, cooperation with specialised service providers and differentialization [sic!] of intervention measures according to some form of risk ranking."[41]

There is clearly scope for military ethicists to engage in both the German and British context, but not only in PME and training. Research, especially comparative research, is much needed to develop a better understanding of the diverse trajectories of extreme right or white supremacist influence in the military and veterans' community, and moreover to assess the very different responses of the government authorities, political representatives the armed forces and civilian society. The latter matters not only in each country's own domestic security context, but, in light of the internationalisation and

39 Mark Townsend, 'Concern for UK security as anti-vaxxer groups evolve towards US-style militias' *The Guardian* (Manchester, 15 January 2022) <https://www.theguardian.com/uk-news/2022/jan/15/concern-for-uk-security-as-anti-vaxxer-groups-evolve-towards-us-style-militias>.

40 'British Soldier Was Jailed For Being Part Of Neo-Nazi Group' *ForcesNet* (BFBS, 12 November 2018) <https://www.forces.net/news/british-soldier-was-jailed-being-part-neo-nazi-group>.

41 Daniel Koehler, *A Threat from Within? Exploring the Link between the Extreme Right and the Military* (2019) International Centre for Counter-Terrorism Policy Brief <https://icct.nl/app/uploads/2019/09/ICCT-Koehler-A-Threat-from-Within-Exploring-the-Link-between-the-Extreme-Right-and-the-Military.pdf>.

diversification of violent extremist networks and groups, that of every states and society in which they are active. Their interdependence leads to interdependent internal security threats, which require co-operation at all levels. Such co-operation is, however, contingent on basic agreement that there is a threat that needs to be addressed and this is not necessarily in place.

In 2021 the Canadian government authorised an official investigation into sexism, racism and extreme right activities in the Canadian armed forces. It found that the Canadian armed forces had 'zero tolerance' policy towards "hateful behaviour", but as is so often the case with such policies, it is not implemented effectively. For example, disciplinary measures were applied inconsistently and at times ill informed. The Canadian Defence Force's filtering process at the time of recruitment is ineffective. Keeping white supremacists from joining the armed forces continues to be a challenge for the Canadian Forces Intelligence Command.

"A thorough review of social media posts from potential recruits is part of the filtering process. But members affiliated with IMVE [Ideologically Motivated Violent Extremist, AE] groups [were] becoming more sophisticated in their use of technology, and they [were] finding ways to be surreptitious in their recruiting interviews. Recruiters [were] not all trained and knowledgeable about methods to detect certain types of behaviour that would indicate affiliation with extremist groups or a penchant for extremist behaviours."[42]

The US military in contrast, "according to retired US Army colonel and former member of the National Security Council Jeff McCausland, 'failed to establish a comprehensive way to screen' out extremists, especially right-wing oriented ones."[43] Moreover there has been strong political resistance to even recognising that a major problem might be developing. In 2019 Koehler found that in "2009, a report by the Department of Homeland Security (DHS)" identified a range of risk factors for extreme right-wing radicalisation of service members.

"These included the election of Barack Obama, a downturn in the economy and large numbers of unemployed veterans returning from combat in Iraq and Afghanistan. The report's publication led to public outcry from Republican politicians, conservative commentators, and veteran associations that ultimately led to its rescindment and the dismantling of the unit responsible for

42 Government of Canada, 'Minister of National Defence Advisory Panel on Systemic Racism and Discrimination: Final Report' (January 2022) <https://www.canada.ca/en/department-national-defence/corporate/reports-publications/mnd-advisory-panel-systemic-racism-discrimination-final-report-jan-2022.html>.

43 Koehler, *A Threat from Within?* (n41).

the assessment. Squashing inopportune reports does little to change the reality they reflect, however. A 2019 poll by the Military Times showed that 22 percent of the surveyed military personnel had seen signs of white nationalism or racist ideology within the armed forces."[44]

The chair of the House Veterans' Committee, Mark Takano, a Democrat, on the other hand warned not only that right-wing extremists had been targeting veterans to recruit them for their cause, something not seen on the left, but also that over the past six years there had been a rise in violence committed by the extreme right much more than from the left of Islamist terrorism.[45] He referenced a report from the Center for Strategic & International Studies which had found that "right-wing extremists perpetrated two-thirds of the attacks and plots in the United States in 2019 and 90% between January 1 and May, 8 2020."[46]

Even today after the January 2021 events there is political resistance to recognising let alone addressing the problem. In July 2022 the Senate Armed Service Committee demanded that the Department of Defense's (DoD) counter-extremism efforts be slashed, because it considered the spending on "exceptionally rare instances of extremism in the military [as] an inappropriate use of taxpayer funds", but the news report highlighted that "the committee approved including that section of the report by [sic!] only the narrowest of margins: 14–12. Every Republican on the committee voted for the motion, and every Democrat voted against it."[47]

The Pentagon had acknowledged the threat after the large number of arrests and convictions of military and ex-military personnel involved in the 6 January 2021 events. In addition Defense Secretary Austin issued an order for military leaders to engage with their service members on these matters and established a Countering Extremist Activity Working Group which reported in December 2021. It pointed out that extremism was "rare", but acknowledged that "'even the actions of a few can have an outsized impact on unit cohesion, morale and readiness.' That is the conclusion of Braniff's [Bill Braniff, Army veteran

44 Koehler, *A Threat from Within?* (n41).

45 Sergio Olmos, ,Recruitment of veterans by extremists may increase, top Democrat warns ' *The Guardian* (Manchester16 January 2022) <https://www.theguardian.com/us-news/2022/jan/16/recruitment-veterans-extremists-mark-takano-democrat>.

46 Seth G. Jones, *The Escalating Terrorism Problem in the United States* (Washington, D.C., Center for International Strategic Studies, 2020) <https://www.csis.org/analysis/escalating-terrorism-problem-united-states>.

47 John M. Donnelly, 'Senate NDAA to Pentagon: "Immediately" halt fight against extremism' *Roll Call* (Washington, DC, 20 July 2022) <https://rollcall.com/2022/07/20/senate-ndaa-to-pentagon-immediately-halt-fight-against-extremism/>.

and director of the University of Maryland's National Consortium for the Study of Terrorism and Responses to Terrorism, or START, AE] research: Extremism among veterans or currently serving military personnel hurts the military's image, not efforts to discuss the issue in the services. Moreover, when people with military ties join extremist groups, they lend an air of bravado to those organizations, helping burnish their bona fides, Braniff and other experts say."[48]

The DoD 2021 report foresaw amongst its key responses to the threat of extremist violence and its prevention an entire line of development around education and training. It did not specify ethics education and training, but its concern for "unit cohesion, morale and readiness" not only touches upon the link between internal and external ethical behaviour, but also leaves plenty of opportunity for ethicists to contribute meaningfully to addressing these multiple challenges and preventing the "outsized impact" just a few can have.

8 Conclusions

The principal conclusion of this analysis has two interdependent parts. Firstly, links between the military and right-wing extremists and white supremacists are growing increasingly complex, are internationally networked and connect underground groups with mainstream politics across several NATO countries. The impact of these developments is a threat to cosmopolitan thought, liberal democracy and its institutions, including the military and the military's nascent diverse and inclusive organisational culture and operational effectiveness, and the civil liberties of its citizens. Secondly, military ethics must be more engaged through research, policy advice and PME in building up a more nuanced understanding of the problem and its varied manifestations, and from here develop effective responses which address the normative and ethical dimensions of these challenges. In conjunction with this engagement, military ethics needs to reflect on its own foundations and underlying assumptions that have shaped its evolution in theory and practice. This will have to include critical assessments of the legacy of the two major wars of the past two decades, Iraq and Afghanistan, and its ramifications for concepts and the practice of military ethics.

The influence of extreme right or white supremacist ideology is corrosive to the professional ethics of the military and its members, if not the rationale for

48 Donnelly (n47).

military ethics as a whole. It demands reflections on the implications of rejecting fundamental tenets on which military ethics in western liberal democracies is based. These include the assumed desirability of a liberal rules based international order which is generated by and shapes international law and imposes constraints on the legitimation of the use of force and the methods of applying force in war.

Over the past three decades there has been a tension between on the one hand a cosmopolitan notion of care and social justice implied in the political narratives on recent wars, the claim that they were necessary in order to protect the lives and freedoms of others, and on the other hand the state-centric communitarian traditional rationale of armed forces, that is, the protection of the nation. The latter was also part of the strategic narrative, but often less prevalent than the cosmopolitan care and social justice aspect. It is, however, the traditional state-centric communitarian rationale which is recognisable to the extreme right, because it resonates with notions of loyalty to the nation, often sanctified through the concept of sacrifice of the individual for the community, and authority through effective organisation and conduct within a strict hierarchical system. These are the armed forces militarised hyper-masculine right-wing extremists want to join.

When the operations in Iraq and especially Afghanistan failed to deliver on the cosmopolitan care and justice narrative, those who had been reluctant to endorse that narrative or even rejected it outright felt especially betrayed. Had they and their fellow soldiers not done their duty and followed legal orders despite their personal misgivings about this narrative? If the eventual outcome of the operations damaged this kind of underlying moral code, it is a possible reason for an individual serving soldier or veteran to seek such meaning elsewhere. In an extreme case that may be in a white supremacist or extreme right-wing community. US veterans proclaiming their ideological agreement with the Taleban upon their retaking of power in Afghanistan in August 2021 can be interpreted in this way.

In-depth reflection on these kinds of tensions between moral codes, ethical frameworks for behaviour and their emotional dimensions is not part of the analytical discourse on contemporary extreme right-wing ideology in and around the armed forces. Social science, history and military ethics can make major contributions to understanding and explaining these dynamics and their ramifications in practice. This in turn can contribute to generating much more finely tuned preventive and ameliorative measures at a political governance level, potentially in intelligence and law enforcement and importantly within the military and its engagement with society. The latter links directly to the key concern of culture change in the armed forces.

The need to examine military ethics in the light of a highly complex extreme right-wing threat to the armed forces and the recent adaptations of military culture to greater diversity and inclusion opens up the opportunity to develop further the relatively limited scholarship on gender-critical analyses of military ethics in theory and practice. This is conceptually relevant and can add valuable insights to the critical analyses of the wars of the past two decades. It can contribute new perspectives on remaining barriers to inclusion, be this of gender, race or LGBTQI+. A comparative assessment of obstacles posed by patriarchal power structures and cultures on the one hand with identification of those set up by right-wing extremist and white supremacist ideologies should furthermore lead to new approaches to more effective inclusion. At the same time, it can raise flags and triggers that can assist in first identifications of individuals who are potentially on the extreme right spectrum.

This ideological and violent threat is both horizontally connected across countries and vertically links the extreme right-wing or white supremacist underground with formal political structures above ground. International co-operation between scholars and practitioners, civilians and member of the armed forces, of any rank, is indispensable. There is a risk that this is becoming a collective security threat to NATO (and EU) countries 'from the inside'. It needs to be met with the kind of commitment to collective security that has traditionally sought to deal with violent threats from the outside.

CHAPTER 8

Teachings of the Catholic Church on Environmental Harm Caused by Military Operations

Loránd Ujházi

1 Introduction

Published on 24 May 2015, Pope Francis' encyclical *Laudato si'* soon came to be regarded as the *Magna Carta* of the Catholic Church on environmental policies.[1,2] It highlights the Pope's commitment to the protection of the environment, already implied by his chosen pontifical name, as Saint Francis of Assisi, an important role model for the Pope, is the patron saint of the poor and the environment. Nevertheless, Francis was not the first Pope to systematically discuss the protection of created things, since several areas of the topic had been subject to theoretical research by Pope Benedict XVI and Pope John Paul II. While these two pontiffs encouraged politicians, academics and business professionals to take this issue seriously, Francis is also the first pope to include environmental matters in almost all of his papal utterances and to have published a comprehensive encyclical about the protection of the environment. Moreover, besides a wide range of security issues, Pope Francis pays close attention to conventional war. However, it is inevitable that the environment and the ethics of war should meet in papal pronouncements at some point. It

1 The publication has been furthered by the Research Institute for the Protection of the Created world" on behalf of Péter Pázmány Catholic University within the framework of the project "Sustainability, resilience – climate change and its social challenges" also supported by the Ministry of Technology and Industry.'

2 Pope Francis, 'Enc. Laudato si' 107 (2015) *Acta Apostolicae Sedis,* 847–945. Gregorio Guitián, 'Pope Francis and Catholic Social Teaching on Ecology Implications for Christians Involved in Business' 20 (2018) *Worldviews* 163–186. Mary Evelyn Tucker – John Grim, 'Four Commentaries on the Pope's Message on Climate Change and Income Inequality' 3 (2016) *The Quarterly Review of Biology* 261–270. Theodore Lai and Cecilia Tortajada, 'The Holy See and the Global Environmental Movements' *Frontiers in Communication publishes,* online:https://www.frontiersin.org/articles/10.3389/fcomm.2021.715900/full.Venugopalan Ittekkot and Eleanor Milne, 'Encyclical Letter "Laudato Si"': A gentle but firm nudge from Pope Francis' 11 (2015) *Environmental Development* 1–5.

 | DOI:10.1163/9789004544314_010

should also be remembered that both modern security policy and the social teaching of the Church view both environmental protection and conventional armed struggle in a complex system. Furthermore, both are intertwined with several other social and security matters. Pope Francis also focuses on both areas, while mentioning issues such as poverty, migration crisis, arms trafficking, arms stockpiling and countless other areas of security.[3] He places particular emphasis on the complete disarmament of nuclear weapons, the use of which in warfare generates enormous environmental damage as well as human suffering.[4] In this paper, I will give a specifically Catholic assessment of the damage caused by military force. I would like to point out that neither war nor the defence of the created world can be understood without the theological and social teaching of the Church. However, the field has a much broader aspect than the categories of the legitimised classical just war tradition. Pope Francis often talks about the need to reconsider the Church's teaching on the just war tradition. Only peace can be just, and the tradition of just war, developed in the fourth century after St Augustine, is untenable.[5] At the same time, in the context of certain armed conflicts, especially the Ukrainian-Russian war, the Pope also uses elements of the just war tradition: the right to self-defence or the defence of one's country is a typical example. He even makes nuanced clarifications, such as the right to buy arms or the link between patriotism and defence.[6] This does not mean that the Pope is wrong when he calls for a reexamination of the just war tradition. Rather, it shows that the ethical evaluation of war cannot be reduced to the just war tradition alone. This is illustrated by the relationship between war and the protection of the created world.

---

3 Paolo Ondarza, 'Pope Francis at the service of peace' https://www.vaticannews.va/en/pope/news/2022-08/pope-francis-appeals-peace-ukraine-war-logic-arms.html.

4 Lan T. Chu, 'God is Not Dead or Violent: The Catholic Church, Just War, and the "Resurgence" of Religion 5 (2012), *Politics and Religion* 419–440. Drew Christiansen, 'The Church Says 'No' to Nuclear Weapons Pastoral and moral implications' English Edition (2017) *La Civiltà Cattolica* 3. Emily Welty, 'The Theological Landscape of the Nuclear Nonproliferation Treaty: the Catholic Church, the World Council of Churches and the Bomb' 7 (2016) *Global Policy*, 396–404.

5 'I believe it is time to rethink the concept of a just war' Courtney Mares https://www.catholicworldreport.com/2022/07/01/pope-francis-i-believe-it-is-time-to-rethink-the-concept-of-a-just-war/.

6 "The motivation is what in a great part qualifies the morality of that act. To defend oneself is not only licit, it's also an expression of love toward one's homeland; whoever doesn't defend something, doesn't love it. Instead, those who defend, love." Pope: Under right conditions, nations may buy weapons for self-defense. https://catholicnews.com/pope-under-right-conditions-nations-may-buy-weapons-for-self-defense/.

2 The Relationship between the Created World and War

According to an often reinterpreted thesis by Lynn White, the term *rule*, which is mentioned in the Biblical creation story (Gen 1:27–28), is the foundation of the Judeo-Christian world's human-centric economic and political systems, which have made significant contributions to contemporary environmental degradation.[7] Admittedly, some small Evangelical Churches do indeed promote human domination instead of focusing on responsibility and moderation.[8] However, this approach is not prevalent amongst mainstream Christian Churches and especially within the Catholic Church. A great illustration of this approach is Pope John Paul II's encyclical *Evangelium Vitae*, which argues that "the dominion granted to man by the Creator is not an absolute power, nor can one speak of a freedom to 'use and misuse', or to dispose of things as one pleases." In the same encyclical, Pope John Paul II also associated the protection of the created world with the "divine prohibition not to eat of the fruit of the tree (cf. Gen 2:16–17)." According to Pope John Paul II's interpretation, "God shows clearly enough that, when it comes to the natural world, we are subject not only to biological laws but also to moral ones, which cannot be violated with impunity."[9] In this case, our level of responsibility ought to be much higher since the use of modern military equipment can induce either direct environmental harm or create security challenges which may have similar consequences.

Another well-known author, Noah Harari argues that the victimisation of nature began when the dominant role of animism was replaced by theistic religions. Animism believed that humans were merely a piece of the mosaic and their life was no more valuable than any other creature. By contrast, agriculture-related religions, including Christianity as suggested by Harari, treat people as pre-eminent beings chosen by their God/gods. Consequently, the role of nature became insignificant.[10] However, from a Christian viewpoint, his argument has a weak point as it separates the created world from theology and transforms nature into a merely matter of sociology or security studies. Under this view, the responsibility of "theistic or farmer religions" is obvious. However, the Judeo-Christian tradition believes that the cause of the disharmony between mankind and the environment, and also of wars, is not the result of divine

7 Lynn White, 'The Historical Roots of Our Ecologic Crisis' 155 (1967) *Science* 1203–1207.
8 James A. Nash, '*Loving Nature: Ecological Integrity and Christian Responsibility*' (Abingdon Press 1991).
9 John Paul II, 'Evangelium vitae' 87 (1995) *Acta Apostolicae Sedis* 446–447.
10 Yuval Noah Harari, '*Homo Deus – A Brief History of Tomorrow*' (Harper 2017) 67–69.

legitimation but the fall of man.[11] As Joachim Gnilka points out, in this tradition, the world is not the product of a cosmic struggle that is a key element of many Oriental origin myths. Neither is the world created by an evil, misanthropic Demiurge, which is a key pillar of Gnostic philosophy.[12] This position is important for two reasons. First, according to mainstream Christianity, the material world was created by God, who is not an evil entity. Second, the world was not created by either a struggle between gods and spiritual beings or a cosmic conflict. Instead, Christians believe that the world is the realisation of God's creative love and that, in the beginning, God, mankind and the created world existed in a harmonic order. Within Judeo-Christian philosophy, war does not occupy a central position, as was the case in the philosophy of Heraclitus,[13] nor is it a natural state, as suggested by Hobbes.[14] Therefore, according to this philosophical tradition, the "original" characteristic of the relationship between humans or humans and nature is harmony.[15] War is an aberration, as is the destruction of nature, and both are attributable to the fall of man. In his message issued on the World Day of Peace in 2009, Pope Benedict XVI described environmental pollution using the following example.[16] "The harmony between the Creator, mankind and the created world, as described by Sacred Scripture, was disrupted by the sin of Adam and Eve, … Human beings let themselves be mastered by selfishness; they misunderstood the meaning of God's command and exploited creation out of a desire to exercise absolute domination over it. But the true meaning of God's original command, as the Book of Genesis clearly shows, was not a simple conferral of authority, but rather a summons to responsibility."[17] Pope Francis was even more straightforward in his 2013 encyclical *Laudato si'*. "The creation accounts in the book of Genesis contain … that human life is grounded in three fundamental and closely intertwined relationships: with God, with our neighbour and with the earth itself. According to the Bible, these three vital relationships have been

11 Marc Gopin, '*Between Eden and Armageddon*' (University Press 2010) 10.
12 Joachim Gnilka, '*Bibel und Koran: Was Sie Verbindet, Was Sie Trennt*' (Verlag Herder 2010) 97.
13 "War is the father and king of all: some he has made gods, and some men; some slaves and some free." Endre, Simon (ed), '*Filozófiatörténeti szöveggyűjtemény*' (Tankönyvkiadó 1960) 23.
14 Thomas Hobbes, '*Leviathan*' (Penguin Classics 2017).
15 '*The Catechism of the Catholic Church*' 198.
16 Benedict XVI, 'If you Want to Cultivate Peace, Protect Creation' https://www.vatican.va/content/benedict-xvi/en/messages/peace/documents/hf_ben-xvi_mes_20091208_xliii-world-day-peace.html.
17 Ibid.

broken, both outwardly and within us. This rupture is sin. ... [we are] refusing to acknowledge our creaturely limitations. This in turn distorted our mandate to "have dominion" over the earth (cf. Gen 1:28), to "till it and keep it" (Gen 2:15). As a result, the originally harmonious relationship between human beings and nature became conflictual (cf. Gen 3:17–19)." For Pope Francis, the protection of created things results from the loss of harmony, which has also created disharmony between humans. The most conspicuous sign of the latter is armed conflict (LS 66). That is why the Jewish-Christian philosophical approach to war includes the treatment of nature. Although this was initially peripheral, the proliferation of devastating modern military technologies has made this connection ever more central. The Catechism of the Catholic Church argues that: "The effectiveness of armaments does not, in itself, legitimise their use in armed conflicts. The commencement of hostilities does not legitimise the use of every type of weapon in a military operation" (Catechism of the Catholic Church 500). Apparently, Catholic social teachings cannot, or ought not, ignore the protection of the created world in the war. This proposition is true even though the issue only became salient relatively recently due to the appearance of modern weapons.[18] The fact that environmental implications of warfare have been disregarded for so long is attributable to several characteristics of Western military culture. This includes its theoretical underpinnings and pragmatism, and not just the Christian interpretation of the creation story. We can summarise the Graeco-Roman military tradition with the following quote from Titus Livius: "cum agris magis cum hominibus urendo populandoqua gesserunt bella."[19] In his time, soldiers not only targeted hostile solders and other human beings but also the enemy's lands and fields.[20] They set houses on fire, felled trees and sacrificed crops grown by their enemies to venerate their gods. As Pliny noted, "It is easy to identify those places where the Roman armies have passed through in Samnium from the amount of destruction they caused and not from the location of their former camps."[21] David J. Hughes also describes how, during wars in antiquity, several animals were deployed on the battlefields.[22] The same researcher also argues that antique

18 Brake Wayne, '*Religious War and Religious Peace in Early Modern Europe*' (Cambridge University Press 2017).

19 T. Liv. VI, 31.

20 Festel De Coulanges, '*The Ancient City*' Imperium Press (2020 Imperium Press) 310.

21 Pliny H. N XXXXV. 12.

22 Donald J Hughes, 'Warfare and Environment in the Ancient World' in Brian Campbell and Lawrence Tritle (ed), '*The Oxford Handbook of Warfare in the Classical World*' (Oxford University Press 2013).

myths like the *Epic of Gilgamesh*, the *Odyssey* or the *Iliad* illustrate that ancient warriors did not care about the protection of animals or the environment. Hughes also provides archaeological evidence that combat in ancient stories alludes to real wars from the same period. The attitudes towards the created world in that age are also illustrated by depictions of Assyrian kings hunting big game, especially lions, in full battle gear.[23] The Athenian general Xenophon published a treatise on hunting.[24] This states that hunting is the best preparation for war and a worthy activity for gods and heroes. In another publication, Hughes also points out that big game hunting was a key pillar of military training within the Roman army and led to the regional spread of certain species.[25] Research by Victor Davis Hanson examined the treatment of agricultural estates in antique military tactics and strategy. This work proves that military forces in antiquity had no qualms about the destruction of crops, cash crops or orchards.[26] The following excerpts from the Bible are quite remarkable. In *Deuteronomy*, the author tells the Hebrews that "If when attacking a town, you have to besiege it for a long time before you capture it, you must not destroy its trees by taking the axe to them: eat their fruit but do not cut them down. Is the tree in the fields human, that you should besiege it too?" (Dt 20:19–20). This passage also suggests that the destruction of the natural environment was common practice for ancient military operations in the Middle East.[27] However, the level of environmental protection in *Deuteronomy* is not comprehensive because the passage only commands its readers to protect those trees which are useful for humanity while: "Any trees, however, which you know are not fruit trees, you may destroy and cut down and use to build siege-works against the hostile town until it falls" (Dt 20: 19–20). The relationship between nature and war appears in other Old Testament books, although not specifically as an instruction for warriors to follow, but rather as a warning against the totalitarian nature of war. A case in point is Jonah 4: 10–11 and the extermination of cedars in Isaiah: "All the lands are at rest and at peace; they break into singing. Even the junipers and the cedars of Lebanon gloat over you and say,

23 Paul Collins, "*Assyrian Palace Sculptures*' (British Museum Press 2008).

24 Xenophon, 'On Hunting' (Warminster 1999).

25 Donald J Hughes, 'Environmental impacts of the Roman economy and social structure: Augustus to Diocletian' in Alf Hornborg and John Robert McNeill and Joan Martinez-Aller (ed), '*Rethinking environmental history: World System history and global environmental change*' (Lanham 2007) 27–40.

26 Victor Davis Hanson, '*Warfare and Agriculture in Classical Greece*' (University of California Press 1998).

27 Joseph Blenkinsopp, 'Deuteronomy' in Raymond E. Brown and Joseph A. Fitzmayer and Roland E. Murphy (ed), '*The New Jerome Biblical Commentary*' (Burns and Oates 1990) 104.

Now that you have been laid low, no one comes to cut us down" (Is 14: 7–8). The prophet Habakkuk even illustrates violence against nature. The violence against Lebanon will come back to haunt you; "the extermination of wild animals will make you afraid" (Hab 2: 17). Other Old Testament verses (Lev 25: 23–24; Psalms 24: 1–2; Psalms 8: 3–8) also mention that man ought to respect created things. However, in these cases, the protection of the environment is inseparable from the ultimate sovereignty of God the Creator. The Bible contains several other descriptions of wars, although the authors do not mention the protection of the created world. However, no archaeological evidence proves that the ancient Israelites actually heeded the instruction in *Deuteronomy* each time they waged war.[28] Rather, the Bible reveals that their wars resulted in a severe destruction of animals, plants and nature at large. Despite their limited historical accuracy, both Biblical descriptions and contemporary military practices suggest that strictly following the rules established by *Deuteronomy* would have hindered the military efficiency of ancient Israelites. The fact that nature and its protection was irrelevant for Israelites is perfectly illustrated by the story of Abimelech, who not only massacred the population of a town he captured but he also "razed the town and sowed it with salt" (Judges 9:45). We find no evidence in the Old Testament that ancient Israelites behaved differently towards nature than their neighbours during their military operations to secure roads, infrastructures or places where armies gathered or when they focused on achieving their tactical and strategic goals.[29] The same is true of waterways, landing sites, observation posts or the diversion of rivers. This is in line with the general military trend from antiquity that the protection of the environment was not a priority in this era. Nevertheless, some antique sources make a contemporary allusion to the protection of nature. Furthermore, an analysis of the Genesis story proves that war and disharmony between people and nature and between humans are all attributable to the fall of man. This is significant since the vast majority of ancient religions which have made a significant influence on Western thinking disregarded environmental factors while evaluating a range of social matters. This includes the conditions for launching a war or adopting a conduct during an armed struggle.

28 Furthermore, we have to question the applicability of *Deuteronomy* on the Israelites' conduct during wars as this book was written after most wars mentioned in the *Bible* have already been completed.

29 Adrienne Mayor, '*Greek fire, poison arrows, and scorpion bombs: Biological and chemical warfare in the ancient world*' (Woodstock 2003) 128–142.

War is not a central topic in the *New Testament*. The ethical interpretation of certain statements by Jesus provide textual support for the cause of peace. It is also plausible to suggest that the theology of the New Testament concludes that the created world is entitled to protection (Mk 16:15; Rom 8:21–22; Rev 21:1). However, the *New Testament* does not give any explicit ethical instructions about the treatment of nature during armed conflicts. Issues of warfare became relevant for Christianity in the third century, when this religion was defining the content of Christian ethics.

3 Technological Weapons, Environmental Harm and Christian Just War

According to Carl von Clausewitz, "more civilised people" have access to more developed armaments than "less civilised ones". Therefore, armed conflicts waged by the former group are much more devastating than those fought by the latter.[30] Clausewitz uses gunpowder as one of his illustrations of this discrepancy.[31] The passage of time has proven the truth of Clausewitz's thesis. The widespread use of highly developed weaponry and techniques during the First World War, including machine guns, improved firepower, quick-firing weapons or chemical weapons, has transformed armed conflict in terms of the scale of human casualties and environmental harm.[32] The environmental harm of mechanised warfare significantly increased during the Second World War[33] and the deployment of nuclear weapons has sparked debates about military ethics. The armed conflicts of the twentieth century (Vietnam War,[34] First Gulf

30 For a comprehensive study of this aspect please consult: Carl von Clausewitz, *On war* (Princeton University Press Princeton 1984) Book 3 Section 15.

31 Carl von Clausewitz, *On war* (Princeton University Press Princeton 1984) Book 3 Section 15.

32 Tait Keller, Destruction of the Ecosystem in International Encyclopedia of the First World War (WWI) 2019. https://encyclopedia.1914-1918-online.net/pdf/1914-1918-Online-destruction_of_the_ecosystem-2014-10-08.pdf. Drew Heiderscheid, 'The Impact of World War One on the Forests and Soils of Europe' (2018) 7 *Ursidae: The Undergraduate Research Journal at the University of Northern Colorado*, 3–1. Dorothee Brantz, 'Environments of Death: Trench Warfare on the Western Front, 1914–1918' in Charles E Closmann (ed), *War and the Environment: Military Destruction in the Modern Age* (College Station 2009) 68–91.

33 Thomas B Robertson, 'The Nature of World War II.' (*Origins Current Events in Historical Perspective Published by the History Departments at the Ohio State University and Miami University* (1 February 2022) <https://origins.osu.edu/connecting-history/nature-world-war-ii-operation-husky-environmentalism-defense-industry>.

34 Gregory Reichberg and Henrik Syse, Protecting the Natural Environment in Wartime: Ethical Considerations (2000) 37 *Journal of Peace Research* 449.

War, Serbia, civil war in Rwanda,[35] conflicts in Syria, Afghanistan, Angola, Sudan,[36] the ongoing war in Ukraine, etc.) have also caused severe ecological damage. Building on the ideas proposed by Stephen Freeland,[37] Gar Smith highlights a major anomaly of international law. He argues that although we have done a great deal to protect human life during armed conflicts, we do not care about nature at all. During wars, we do not protect our forests, rivers, oceans and atmosphere.[38] This is a worrying development since the mechanisation of war has created a situation where achieving our military objectives carries an ever-growing environmental price tag. All of this seems to support the argument that international legislation has been incapable of stopping ecological damage during military conflicts.[39] In Christian ethics, the best-known theory about war is called the just war tradition, which provides guidelines about launching, waging and terminating military action. However, the just war tradition is not a comprehensive, monolithic construct. Instead, it is a patchwork of theories proposed by various Christian scholars who reflected on the wars, security challenges and new weapons which arose in their respective historical periods. Generally speaking, the Catholic just war ethic has articulated issues related to the environment only in the context of modern military power and destructive weapons. However, it is worth pointing out that not only the content of the just war tradition, but also the method of examining the issue have changed over time. Although (Catholic) theorists have built on each other's theories, they have adapted their arguments to their own historical times and to the expectations of the Church and the Pope. The volume by Daniel R. Brunstetter and Cian O'Driscoll provides a deep insight into the work of the theorists of the Catholic just war tradition, among others.[40] It is not the purpose of this paper to repeat the arguments of the book, but only to point out that there is a difference in elaboration of depth, content and approach

35 Karl Mathiesen, What's the environmental impact of modern war? *The Guardian* (1 February 2022) https://www.theguardian.com/environment/2014/nov/06/whats-the-environmental-impact-of-modern-war.

36 James Tasamba 'Armed conflicts affect environment and wildlife: Experts' https://www.aa.com.tr/en/africa/armed-conflicts-affect-environment-and-wildlife-experts/1636318.

37 Steven Freeland, *'Addressing the Intentional Destruction of the Environment during Warfare under the Rome Statute of the International Criminal Court (18) (Supranational Criminal Law)*. UK' (Intersentia 2015).

38 Gar Smith, *'The war and environment reader'* (Just World Books 2017) 326.

39 Gregory Reichberg and Henrik Syse, 'Protecting the Natural Environment in Wartime: Ethical Considerations' 37 (2000) *Journal of Peace Research* 449.

40 Daniel R. Brunstetter and Cian O'Driscoll (ed), *'Just War Thinkers: From Cicero to the 21st Century'* (War, Conflict and Ethics), (Routledge 2018).

between St Augustine,[41] St. Thomas Aquinas,[42] and Maister Gratianus[43] or Francisco de Vittoria,[44] and so on. A look at the context of the created world and war shows how war has been assessed as an increasingly closed and legal category. The authors concerned tried to cover all aspects of war with the legal categories of just war. However, the first authors, like Augustine, did not yet set up the field of just war with legal categories[45] but, as Herbert Deane underlines, he treated all areas with the freedom of preachers,[46] including the question of war. Whether or not nature appears within the category of just war, we cannot ignore Augustine's deep cosmology. For theological reasons, this is one of the best-developed areas of the philosophy of Agustin. It is the subject of both his great works (*Confessions*, *City of God*) and his homilies. Augustine dedicated a separate book called *On Genesis* to the order of creation.[47] St Augustine's cosmology has been the subject of many excellent theological analyses.[48] Here I would just like to mention that in Augustine, and then in the Western Christian tradition, the creation of the world is creation from nothing (creatio ex nihilo), most deeply connected to the debate of the cosmic struggle between good and evil. Unlike other schools of thought (Manichaeism, Middle Platonism), early Christian thinkers were committed to the idea that the created world is a manifestation of God's goodness and a gift from God. Therefore, human responsibility to take care of it, it cannot be neglected in the case of wars, no matter how well developed this area is in the just war ethic itself. Rory Cox rightly says that it is to Gratian's credit that the principles of just war were

---

41 James Turner Johnson, 'St. Augustine' in Daniel R. Brunstetter and Cian O'Driscoll (ed), *'Just War Thinkers: From Cicero to the 21st Century'* (War, Conflict and Ethics), (Routledge 2018) 21–34.

42 Gregory M. Reichberg, 'Thomas Aquinas' in Daniel R. Brunstetter and Cian O'Driscoll (ed), *'Just War Thinkers: From Cicero to the 21st Century (War, Conflict and Ethics)'* (Routledge 2018) 50–64.

43 Rory Cox, 'Gratian' in Daniel R. Brunstetter and Cian O'Driscoll (ed), *'Just War Thinkers: From Cicero to the 21st Century' (War, Conflict and Ethics)'* (Routledge 2018) 34–50.

44 Alex Bellamy, 'Francisco de Vittoria' Aquinas' in Daniel R. Brunstetter and Cian O'Driscoll (ed), *'Just War Thinkers: From Cicero to the 21st Century (War, Conflict and Ethics)'* (Routledge 2018) 77–92.

45 Jonh Mark Mattox, *'Saint Augustine and the Theory of Just War'* (Continuum 2006) 1.

46 Herbert A. Deane, *'The Political and Social Ideas of St. Augustine'* (University Press 1963).

47 For a critical edition see: Augustine *'On Genesis: Two books on Genesis against the Manichees. On the literal interpretation of Genesis, an unfinished book'* (Catholic University of America Press 1991).

48 William A. 'Christian, Augustine on the Creation of the World' 46 (1953) *The Harvard Theological Review* 1–25. Thomas E. Clarke, 'St. Augustine and Cosmic Redemption' 19 (1958) *Theological Studies* 133–164. John O'Meara, Saint Augustine's Understanding of the Creation and Fall' 10 (1984) *The Maynooth Review* 56–62.

widely disseminated and given legal language.[49] But let us add that it was also thanks to Gratian, and to the great jurists of the period, such as Raymond of Penyafort or Francisco de Vitoria, that war was brought within a legal framework. To this were added the medieval legal rules of the Church, such as the treuga dei, which also bore the characteristics of "legal institutions". Neither scholasticism nor St Thomas changed this significantly, since Thomas himself, in his treatise on the short war, relies as much, if not more, on the jurists of the time than on the philosophy of St Augustine.[50] Thus, with regard to the early Christian authors, an important conclusion can be drawn. The theological and historical impact of these authors, especially Augustine, on the created world and war is much deeper than simply looking at it through the tradition of just war.[51] Ghislain Lafont makes an important comment on the theological and canon law history of the Catholic Church. According to Lafont, in the Middle Ages, when the great theological debates were over, the Church's interest turned towards canon law and institutional regulation.[52] They were thinking in terms of legal systems, and just as they sought precision in private law, especially in contracts, because of urbanisation and the growth of trade, so too were the institutions of the Church and social teaching, including war. Many centuries of juridical thinking have made it difficult to escape from the categories of just war that promise safe categories. Mark Woods underlines that there is much more to the environment and war than placing nature within the classical just war tradition. Woods also lists modern attempts to do so, pointing out their imperfections.[53] He is also right merely on the grounds of natural logical reasoning. For example, according to Marcus Hedahl, Scott Clark and Michael Beggins, it would be worth incorporating the environmental impacts of military action in the proportionality and innocent protection aspects of the just war tradition.[54] Whether we treat nature as an innocent non-combatant party

49 Rory Cox, op. cit 34–35.

50 Gregory M. Reichberg, op. cit, 50–64.

51 Mark Rochelle Ferraren Renacia, Contemporary Ecology and Augustine on Creation' 94 (2019) *Estudios eclesiásticos* 363–402.

52 Ghislain Lafont, 'Histoire théologique de l'Église catholique' (Le cerf 1994).

53 Mark Woods, 'The nature of war and peace: Just War thinking, environmental ethics, and environmental justice, Michael W. Brough and John W. Lango and Harry Van Der Linden, '*Rethinking the Just War Tradition*' (State University of New York Press 2007) 17–35.

54 Marcus Hedahl, and Scott Clark and Michael Beggins, 'The Changing Nature of the Just War Tradition: How Our Changing Environment Ought to Change the Foundations of Just War Theory' 19 (2017) *Public Integrity* 429–430 See forth Cian O'Driscoll, 'Re-Writing the Just War Tradition Just War in Classical Greek Political Thought and Practice' 59 (2015) *International Studies Quarterly* 1–10.

or stick to the principle of proportionality and concentrate on limiting the level of environmental impairment during military operations to the necessary level is a question that has remained unanswered.[55] Do we protect nature during wars if we choose either of the two options? Do we look at nature as an innocent being that is unable to flee or bear arms? The answer is probably in the negative. The restoration of damage caused by war is another significant unresolved issue. How and when can we undo the harm caused by chemical weapons, radioactive materials or mechanised warfare? Often such process is long, sometimes taking centuries. In other cases, the consequences of war are irreversible.[56] This is the logic behind the argument that it is difficult to consider the relationship between war and ecological damage in the just war tradition alone. From a theological point of view, we have already alluded to the relationship between war devastation and the created world on the basis of creation theology. The fact that ecclesiastical legal thinking was never really effective in the context of the war is another matter. Even today it is unlikely that during an armed conflict either side would refrain from using a specific weapon or tactic merely due to potential ecological hazards. Nevertheless, some international organisations, like NATO,[57] consider the environmental consequences of military operations in their policy planning. However, nobody can guarantee that the opposing side will behave the same way.[58] The ethical aspects of wars have always been subordinated to the advantage, whether tactical, strategic or technological, on the battlefield. A study by Péter Erdő shows that, even in the Middle Ages, the Church's attempts to punish the use of certain weapons were ineffective merely because decision-makers were unwilling the relinquish the practical advantage that the use of ethically controversial weapons gave them on the battlefield.[59] As a rule, it was not the environmental damage caused by the new weapons that church documents highlighted at the time. It is worth noting, however, that some earlier scholars had proposed the

---

55 Gregory Reichberg and Henrik Syse, Protecting the Natural Environment in Wartime: Ethical Considerations from the Just War Tradition' 37 (2000) *Journal of Peace Research* 449–468.

56 For a comprehensive survey about the long-term consequences of chemical weapon usage see Giovanni Tortorici and Francesco Fiorito, 'Building in post-war environments' 180 (2017) *Procedia Engineering* 1093–1102.

57 NATO/SPS Short Term Project, 'Environmental Aspects of Military Compounds' https://www.nato.int/science/topical_ws/eamc/283-final_report_Compounds_phaseII.pdf.

58 Jasper Humphreys and M. L. R. Smith, 'War and wildlife: the Clausewitz connection' 87 (2011) *International Affairs (Royal Institute of International Affairs 1944-)* 121–142.

59 Péter Erdő, 'Az íjászok és hajítógép-kezelők büntetése. Adalékok a kánonjogi esetmegoldás módszeréhez a kései középkorban' 2 (2008) *Magyar Sion* 23.

inclusion of some environmental elements into the just war concept. One such example can be found in Francisco de Vitoria's *De Indis* (1532). In this volume, the destruction of orchards and oil groves becomes a reason which may justify going to war.[60] Furthermore, according to Hugo Grotius, the poisoning of the soil, similarly to the poisoning of a man, also legitimises the decision to go to war.[61] But here, also, legal thinking became dominant and war was seen from the human rather than the environmental point of view. Nevertheless, Mark Woods is also right that it is simplistic to divide the just war tradition into two groups: the antropocentric and the environmentally conscious approach. While the representatives of the first group subordinate the environment to military objectives, the second group seeks the rights of nature in the triple categories of tradition: jus ad bellum, jus in bello, jus post bellum. Woods has summarised in eight points the types of environmental damage that the use of military force can result in. All I would like to highlight is that the list, which will presumably be expanded as new technologies emerge, shows that environmental damage caused by military force always has a negative impact on people and communities.[62] Therefore, as Noam Chomsky and Laray Polk rightly observe, an environmental catastrophe is also a human catastrophe. But what this really shows that not only is the two-category approach (anthropocentric and environment-centric) a simplification, but also an attempt to categorise the environmental factors caused by the armed forces in the just war tradition.[63] The field of environment and war raises many more and more complex questions than theories of just war can answer.[64] Not to mention that

---

60 Francisco de Vitoria, '*Indis*' 54. sec. 1532.

61 Hugo Grotius, '*De Jure Belli ac Pacis. On the Law of War and Peace*' (Cambridge University Press 2020)2, 1.

62 Stockholm International Peace Research Institute (SIPRI), *Warfare in a Fragile World: Military Impact on the Human Environment* (Taylor and Francis 1980), Arthur H. Westing, (ed), Explosive Remnants of War: Mitigating the Environmental Effects (Taylor and Francis 1985). Susan D. Lanier-Graham, '*The Ecology of War: Environmental Impacts of Weaponry and Warfare*' (Walker and Company 1993). Jay E. Austin and Carl E. Bruch, (ed), '*The Environmental Consequences of War: Legal, Economic, and Scientific Perspectives*' (Cambridge University Press 2000). Rosalie Bertell, '*Planet Earth: The Latest Weapon of War*' (The Women's Press 2000). Mark A. Harwell, '*Nuclear Winter: The Human and Environmental Consequences of Nuclear War*' (Springer-Verlag 1984). Lydia Dotto, '*Planet Earth in Jeopardy: Environmental Consequences of Nuclear War*' (John Wiley & Sons 1986).

63 Noam Chomsky and Laray Polk, '*Nuclear War and Environmental Catastrophe*' (Seven Stories Press 2013) 7.

64 Braden Allenby, 'Emerging technologies and just war theory' in Fritz Allhoff, Nicholas G. Evans and Adam Henschke (ed), '*Routledge Handbook of Ethics and War, Just war theory in the twenty-first century*' (Routledge 2013) 289–301.

there are areas of armed forces and environment that fall outside the categories of just war. Even many non-combat related activities, like the development of military technology or carrying out standard peacetime activities have a significant ecological impact.[65] A great deal of rare metals, minerals or water is often required during armament production. Furthermore, the use and maintenance of military aircraft, vehicles and infrastructure also entails significant CO_2 emissions and a high environmental load. Moreover, the testing of military equipment and military training activities in general often take place at ecologically fragile locations so these activities can pose a threat to biodiversity. Even countries that have laws regulating the process might not follow these guidelines, which could otherwise make environmentally friendly disposal possible, due to the lack of funds. Accidents during military activity also create problems since these litter the ocean floor with nuclear ordnance or nuclear reactors or may poison wide swathes of territory.[66] Finally, we must not forget the social consequences of arms races. This may entail impoverishment or the weakening of the safety net.[67] Considering all of these facts, we have to agree with Pope Francis when he said we need to rethink elements of the classical just war tradition. The damage caused to the environment and its prevention reinforces the security paradigm that the security challenges of our time are far more complex than can be assessed using a single model.

4 The Road to Pope Francis in the Field of Protecting the Created World

Woods basically follows contemporary theorists of the just war tradition (Syse, Drucker, Duane, Walzer, O'Brien, Reichberg, Finnis) in concluding that it is hard to apply the elements of the just war tradition when considered in the context of modern warfare and environmental harms. Zoltán Turgonyi notes that there are logical elements of natural law that are acceptable from a merely

65 The Military's Impact on the Environment: A Neglected Aspect of the Sustainable Development Debate A Briefing Paper for States and Non-Governmental Organisations International Peace Bureau, Geneva August 2002. (30/01/2022) online: https://www.ipb.org/wp-content/uploads/2017/03/briefing-paper.pdf.

66 Paper for States and Non-Governmental Organisations International Peace Bureau, Geneva August 2002. https://www.ipb.org/wp-content/uploads/2017/03/briefing-paper.pdf.

67 Joseph J. Fahey, 'The Catholic Church and the Arms Race' 22 (1979) *Worldview* 38–41.

rational point of view.[68] Thus, for example, without theological reasoning, a purely utilitarian approach can lead us to the conclusion that the development, deployment and destruction of modern military forces can nowadays result in environmental damage that threatens the survival of human communities. More specifically, Jerald Richards, among others, draws a similar conclusion from an ethical approach to war,[69] and David A. Hoekema[70] describes the destructive power of modern weapons, especially nuclear weapons.[71] Clearly, the development of military technology and destructive force has had a repercussion on philosophical thinking about war. John Finnis specifically refers to Catholic history, pointing out that since the Catholic doctrine of the ethics of war was born as a complex system, it has always provided a certain margin of manoeuvre for individual theorists. He demonstrated it, for example, by the summary of Alexander of Hales and Thomas Aquinas, who linked their ethics of war to other points.[72] Accordingly, it is also fair to say that Catholic theology has not only the opportunity but also the duty to integrate the newly emerging security challenges into the social teaching of the Catholic Church. Gregory M. Reichberg highlights the fact that, although the rethinking of the just war theory is associated with Michael Waltzer and Paul Ramsey, the Catholic side had already begun to rethink the doctrine between the two wars.[73] Although this was not yet an environmental issue, it was indicative of the need to rethink the rules for the use of military force in the light of changing technical means. However, it is not only the different elements that need to be noted, but also the fact that there is a certain continuity in the Church's just war tradition. Martin Schlag points out in the context of the Church's social teaching that there are constant theological elements that do not change and new aspects

68 Turgonyi Zoltán, '*Természetjogállam*' (Kairosz Kiadó 2021) 20–21 (English version in process).

69 Jerald Richards, 'Walzer's Just War Theory and Limited Nuclear First Strikes' 15 (1983) *Peace Research* 64–70.

70 David A. Hoekema, Morality, Just War, and Nuclear Weapons: An Analysis of "The Challenge Of Peace", 67 (1984) *Soundings: An Interdisciplinary Journal* 359–378. See also Noam Chomsky and Laray Polk, op. cit.

71 David A. Dombrowski, 'The Death of the Just War Theory' 13 (1981) *Peace Research*, 135–144, Warren Steikraus, 'Does it Make any Sense to Talk About a 'Just War'?' 5 (1974) *Journal of Social Philosophy* 8–11.

72 John Finnis, 'The Ethic of War and Peace in the Catholic Natural Law Tratdition' In John Aloysius Coleman (ed), '*Christian Political Ethics*' (Princeton University Press 2007) 18–19.

73 Gregory M. Reichberg, 'Reframing the Catholic Understanding of Just War Two Contrasting Approaches in the Interwar Period' 46 (2018), *Journal of Religious Ethics* 570–596. For example: Robert Regout, '*La doctrine de la guerre juste de Saint Augustin à nos jours*' (Regout 1934).

that develop in relation to the current social situation.[74] Fred van Iersel has dedicated a monograph to the Catholic Church's ethics of war, presenting some of the elements of change and also drawing a conclusion for the future.[75] The fact is that the direct discussion of war and the environment appeared relatively late in the Church's statements[76] but, as seen above, it did not mean that the Church negated nature, since it was an integral part of Catholic theology. Twentieth-century popes directly criticised the mechanised wars which raged during their pontificates. In John Pollard's biography of Pope Benedict XV, several chapters deal with the pope's attempts to bring an end to the Great War and his charitable activities using relevant papal and Holy See sources.[77] Although Pope Benedict XV never overtly talked about the protection of the environment, his statement that "the flourishing Europe, driven by a universal madness, is committing a real suicide" also applied to nature. The First World War not only claimed the lives of millions of people but also radically transformed Europe's biodiversity, forests and soils.[78] Although Benedict XV's calls for peace focused on people and communities, mankind is inseparable from its environment and the created world. This fact remains true even though these elements are not explicitly mentioned in papal communications.

The Second World War caused such severe and visible environmental damage that the Catholic Church's official communications started to openly mention the link between war and the created world. Afterwards, the harm related to the deployment of high-technology weapons became a mainstay

---

74 Martin Schlag, 'Political Life: Peace, Freedom, and Justice in Society' In Martin Schlag (ed), *'Handbook of Catholic Social Teaching A Guide for Christians in the World Today'* (The Catholic University of America Press 2017) 97–101. See alos Paul Josef Cardinal Cordes, 'Paradigm Shift in the Social Doctrine of the Church: From Rerum Novarum (1891) to Caritas in Veritate (2009)' in Martin Schlag – Juan Andrés Mercado (ed), *'Free Markets and the Culture of Common Good'* (Springer 2012) 83–93. Bryan J. Hehir, 'John Paul II, Continuity and Change in the Social Teaching of the Church' In Charles E. Curran and Richard A. McCormick (ed), *'Readings in Moral Theology 5: Official Catholic Social Teaching'* (Paulist 1986) 247–263.

75 Fred van Iersel, *'The Future of Just War Theory: A Catholic Approach'* (Forum Religion & Sozialkultur 2020).

76 David D. Corey and Josh King, 'Pacem in Terris and the Just War Tradition: A Semicentennial Reconsideration' 12 (2013) *Journal of Military Ethics* 142–161.

77 John P. Pollard, *'The Unknown Pope Benedict XV (1914–1922) and the Pursuit of Peace'* (Geoffrey Chapman 1999) Especially chapters 4, 5 and 6.

78 Tait Keller, 'Destruction of the Ecosystem' in 'International Encyclopedia of the First World War (WW1)' https://encyclopedia.1914-1918-online.net/pdf/1914-1918-Online-destruction_of_the_ecosystem-2014-10-08.pdf. Dorothee Brantz, 'Environments of Death: Trench Warfare on the Western Front, 1914–1918' in Charle E. Closmann (ed), *'War and the Environment: Military Destruction in the Modern Age*, (College Station 2009) 68–91.

of Catholic ethical examinations of war. An early example was Pope Pius XII's warning the world about the potential military uses of nuclear energy in 1943, two years before the deployment of the first nuclear weapon. Then, in his 1954 Easter Day Address, he called for the total abolition of nuclear weapons due to their extremely destructive nature. The Pope's rationale for the ban was that the use of this weapon causes unimaginable human suffering, inflicts bodily deformities and renders large territories uninhabitable.[79] Furthermore, Pius XII argued, the devastation and pollution caused by the deployment of nuclear weapons will also necessarily affect those peoples and nations who have decided to use such weapons.[80] *Pacem in terris*, Pope John XXIII's landmark encyclical in this field, also mentions that modern "wars cause ... great fields of ruin" and "there is reason to fear that the very testing of nuclear devices for war purposes can, if continued, lead to severe danger for various forms of life on earth."[81] Furthermore, these weapons have such a "terrifying destructive force ... in this age, which boasts of its atomic power, that it no longer makes sense to maintain that war is a fit instrument with which to repair the violation of justice."[82] The starting point of John XXIII's political philosophy was international cooperation based on the establishment of peace. Already in his first radio address, he drew attention to the responsibility of international diplomacy, which should be at the service of mutual peace building rather than of the arms race.[83] Brian Kane notes that John XXIII's philosophy of peace and related activities are in many ways related to those of Popes Pius XI and Pius XII (peace in the sense of St Augustine, Christmas messages of peace, etc.).[84] The great merit of John XXIII, however, is that the interpretation of war is brought back into the social complexity in which the Church originally valued it.[85] What is new about John XXIII and the Council is not that the Pope felt competent to assess the broad security challenges in a global context. This was done by his predecessors. Rather, the merit of John XXIII is that he has capacitated the Holy See to move global peace and the

79 Holy See Mission, 'The Holy See on the Abolition of Nuclear Weapons' https://holysee mission.org/ contents/ statements/55e34d381107a0.55385271.php.

80 Gregory S. Kavka, 'Hobbes's War of all against all' 1 (1983) *Ethics* 306.

81 Pope John XXIII, Enc. 'Pacem in terris' n. III. 55. (1963) *Acta Apostolicae Sedis* 257–304.

82 Ibid. n. 127.

83 Pope John XXIII, 'Hac trepida hora' 50 (1958) *Acta Apostolicae Sedis* 839–841.

84 Brian M. Kane, 'John XXIII and Just Cause for Modern War' 80 (1999) *New Blackfriars* 56–72.

85 David D. Corey and Josh King, 'Pacem in Terris and the Just War Tradition: A Semicentennial Reconsideration' 12 (2013) *Journal of Military Ethics* 142–161.

universal common good forward through its own instruments.[86] The military means used in the Second World War and further developed in the Cold War could not be evaluated only through the legalised categories of just war. John XXIII recognised this and passed it on to his successors, Paul VI, John Paul II, Benedict XVI and the current Pope. In 1967, in a speech delivered at the United Nations, Pope Paul VI alluded to the duality which is inseparable from the fact that "the individual has access to ever more powerful tools which make him capable of causing either more destruction or noble advancement."[87] It is difficult not to interpret this quote as an allusion to the greatest security challenge of the Cold War, the use of nuclear or any other weapons of mass destruction. This approach is underlined by *Gaudium et spes*, the pastoral constitution of the Second Vatican Council. It uses the term *scientific weapons* when talking about weapons of mass destruction (GS 80).[88] *Gaudium et spes* also asserts that "acts of war involving these weapons can inflict massive and indiscriminate destruction, thus going far beyond the bounds of legitimate defense. Indeed, if the kind of instruments which can now be found in the armouries of the great nations were to be employed to their fullest, an almost total and altogether reciprocal slaughter of each side by the other would follow, not to mention the widespread devastation that would take place in the world and the deadly after effects that would be spawned by the use of weapons of this kind" (GS 80). In his encyclical *Octogesima Adveniens*, Paul VI mentions environment pollution as one of the new social problems. He states that "Man is suddenly becoming aware that by an ill-considered exploitation of nature he risks destroying it and becoming in his turn the victim of this degradation."[89] Paul VI presents environmental problems in all their complexity, such as "chemical pollution, new diseases" and here he also mentions "total destructive devices." He refers to the effects on the whole human family, global disasters, i.e. transboundary effects. It is significant that modern weapons of destruction and environmental pollution are mentioned together. In this context, Mary Elsbernd has pointed out that the encyclical also reflects the conceptual shift in Paul VI's understanding

86 John F. Kobler, 'The Influence of Pacem in Terris' in John F. Kobler, '*Vatican II and Phenomenology Reflections on the Life – World of the Church*' (1975 Nijhoff Publishers).

87 Paul VI, 'Discors' 57 (1967) *Acta Apostolicae Sedis* 885.

88 Lóránd Ujházi, 'Nuclear Deterrence in the Reflections of the Catholic Church' 16 (2020) *Iustum Aequum Salutare* 105–120.

89 Pope Paul VI, Apostolic letter 'Octogesims Adveniens' 63 (1971) *Acta Apostolicae Sedis* 416–417.

of security: violence, war and genocide highlighted the complexity of security challenges, as highlighted by *Octogesima Adveniens*.[90]

Pope John Paul II is the pontiff who underlined a direct link between the application of military force and the protection of created things. On the World Day of Peace on 1st January 1990, he delivered a landmark speech entitled *Peace with God the Creator, Peace with all of Creation*.[91] In this speech, the Pope argued that "Today, any form of war on a global scale would lead to incalculable ecological damage. But even local or regional wars, however limited, not only destroy human life and social structures, but also damage the land, ruining crops and vegetation as well as poisoning the soil and water. The survivors of war are forced to begin a new life in very difficult environmental conditions, which in turn create situations of extreme social unrest, with further negative consequences for the environment." The Pope also discusses the fact that the survivors of wars are forced to restart their lives in harsh environments. These factors may spawn several unwanted circumstances like extreme levels of social unrest and further environmental harm. Finally, John Paul II highlights the "risks of chemical, bacteriological and biological warfare ... capable of altering the balance of nature."[92] What makes this declaration extremely significant is that it openly brings together several war-, peace-and nature-related issues.[93] It was at Pope John Paul II's request that the Pontifical Council for Justice and Peace compiled the *Compendium of the Social Doctrine of the Church*. The *Compendium* dedicates two chapters, Chapters 14 and 15, to matters of environmental protection and peace. The *Compendium* also points out that nuclear disarmament (509) and the ban on chemical and nuclear warfare tests are closely related goals. Furthermore, the *Compendium* rejects "any act of war aimed indiscriminately at the destruction of entire cities or extensive areas (...)."[94] The *Compendium* does not, however, examine in depth the relationship between military operations and ecological damage. The *Compendium* was published by Pope Benedict XVI, who issued multiple warnings about the negative consequences of modern warfare. In his 2009 message on the World

---

90 Mary Elsbernd, 'What Ever Happened to Octogesima Adveniens?' 56 (1995) *Theological Studies* 41.

91 Pope John Paul II. 'Discors. 1990. I. 1.' https://www.vatican.va/content/john-paul-ii/en/messages/peace/documents/hf_jp-ii_mes_19891208_xxiii-world-day-for-peace.html.

92 Ibid. n. 12.

93 Scott C Powell, '*An Environmental Ethic for the End of the World: An Ecological Midrash on Romans 8:19–22*' (Cambridge 2019) 7.

94 Pontifical Council for Justice and Peace, '*Compendium of the Social Doctrine of the Church*' https://www.vatican.va/roman_curia/pontifical_councils/justpeace/documents/rc_pc_justpeace_doc_20060526_compendio-dott-soc_en.html n. 509.

Day of Peace, Pope Benedict XVI discussed ruthlessness, wars, international and local conflicts and terrorism and mentioned humanity's transgressions against nature.[95] In section 51 of his encyclical *Caritas in veritate*, he argues that "Moreover, how many natural resources are squandered by wars! Peace in and among peoples would also provide greater protection for nature. The hoarding of resources, especially water, can generate serious conflicts among the peoples involved. Peaceful agreement about the use of resources can protect nature and, at the same time, the well-being of the societies concerned."[96] Pope Benedict also suggested that, in a globalised world, nation-states are not powerful enough to achieve the above-mentioned goals. What is neededinternational actors that are independent of nation-states.[97] Bernard Laurent notes that Benedict XVI, in addition to the importance he attributes to international organisations in addressing major social issues, also refers to the dysfunctionality of these same organisations, most clearly articulated in the broader context of security challenges.[98]

Pope John Paul II and especially Pope Benedict XVI found the issue of environmental protection, war and scientific weapons quite significant. Admittedly, while opposing war and violence, previous popes did not exclude the moral permissibility of using military force.[99] Pope Francis followed suit by building a complex theory upon a commitment to total disarmament and the radical protection of the ecology.

5 Pope Francis' Protection of the Created World and War

"Today we have pleaded for the holy gift of peace. We have prayed that consciences will be mobilized to defend the sacredness of human life, to promote peace between peoples and to care for creation, our common home."[100] These

95 Benedict XVI, Enc., 'Caritas in veritate' 101 (2009) *Acta Apostolicae Sedis* 687–688.

96 Vincent Strand, 'On Method, Nature and Grace in Caritas in Veritate' 15 (2017) *Nova et vetera* 835–852.

97 Maryann O. Keating and Barry P. Keating and Jesse H. Jones, 'Benedict XVI as Social Realist in Caritas in Veritate' 14 (2011) *Journal of Markets & Morality* 350.

98 Bernard Laurent, 'Caritas in Veritate as a Social Encyclical: A Modest Challenge to Economic, Social, and Political Institutions' 71 (2010) *Theological Studies* 515–544.

99 John Langan, 'The Elements of St. Augustine's Just War Theory' 12 (1984) *The Journal of Religious Ethics* 34.

100 Pope Francis: '*Address of the Holy Father*' https://www.vatican.va/content/francesco/en/speeches/2016/september/documents/papa-francesco_20160920_assisi-preghiera-pace.html.

words were uttered by Pope Francis in the Basilica of Saint Francis in Assisi on 20th September 2016 at an international ecumenical meeting. This was not the only occasion when Pope Francis connected the issue of war and the protection of created world.

In 2015, the Pope stressed to the military chaplains the importance of international humanitarian law, which seeks to ban weapons that cause terrible and senseless suffering to combatants, not to mention the very serious damage caused to the natural and cultural environment.[101] But the key declarative document which examines the interrelatedness of war, peace and the social teaching of the Catholic Church is *Laudato si'*. It provides a great illustration of the complex relations that exist between war and the ecology: "War always does grave harm to the environment and to the cultural riches of peoples, risks which are magnified when one considers nuclear arms and biological weapons. Despite the international agreements which prohibit chemical, bacteriological and biological warfare, the fact is that laboratory research continues to develop new offensive weapons capable of altering the balance of nature" (LS 57). Other sections of this encyclical evaluate the relationship between the protection of the created world and war from various other standpoints (LS 66; 104; 198; 200 and 225). Here the Pope discusses the role of economic institutions, financial systems, poverty, social structures and arms trading in this context. Interestingly, the content of this "green" encyclical suggests that, to thoroughly and comprehensively study any social or security issue, we must necessarily rely on an interdisciplinary dialogue between various sciences.[102] The same concept is found in the apostolic constitution *Veritatis gaudium*, which regulates Catholic universities.[103] One of the appendixes of this document lists those academic disciplines that ought to be included in the portfolio of Catholic universities. It contains either Peace Studies or the complex study

101 Pope Francis: https://www.catholicsun.org/2015/10/27/chaplains-must-assist-military-traumatized-by-war-pope-says/.

102 Ottmar Edenhofer, '*Seven Statements on Pope Francis's encyclical "Laudato Si". Potsdam-Institut für Klimafolgenforschung*' https://www.mcc-berlin.net/fileadmin/data/pdf/Publikationen/In_den_Medien/Seven_Statements_Laudato_Si_Edenhofer.pdf.

103 Pope Francis, Const. Ap., 'Veritatis gaudium' 4. n. https://www.vatican.va/content/francesco/en/apost_constitutions/documents/papa-francesco_costituzione-ap_20171208_veritatis-gaudium.html. József Padányi, 'National defence research on the effects of climate change', 23 (2013) *Hadtudomány: A Magyar Hadtudományi Társaság Folyóirata* 30–40. Job Kozhamthadam, Vatican II on Science & Technology' 63 (2007) *Revista Portuguesa de Filosofia* 609–629.

of various ecological issues.[104] Pope Francis has also discussed war and the protection of the created world in his encyclical *Fratelli tutti*. This document synthesized various elements proposed by Pope Francis' ideals into a structured whole. According to Pope Francis, wars have such dramatically negative ecological consequences[105] that they can never be justified either by the classical or reformed interpretations of the just war theory. If we accept the key paradigm of the encyclical by which we all are brothers and sisters and that the Earth is our shared home, then we can never forget that modern wars do not care about national borders and endanger our shared home.[106] The logical conclusion of these positions, as expressed by Pope Francis several times before the publication of *Fratelli tutti*, is that war can never be just and we must be committed to the protection of the ecology and total nuclear disarmament.[107] However, *Fratelli tutti* is the first papal communication where these three elements all appear together to set up a new framework. The environmental and global consequences of wars are examined in sections 259–262 of the encyclical. It makes it clear that globalisation has negative impacts on the ecology, which may be invisible but are no longer regional. Instead, they frequently threaten the future of the globe as a whole. Moreover, it makes it clear that the previously used to legitimise defensive wars, even within the Catechism of the Catholic Church, are no longer applicable. This change happened because these arguments have continuously been misused, especially in the recent past, by various parties to underpin their assertions that their military operations constituted just defensive wars. The same actors also relied on

---

104 Pope Francis, Const. Ap., *'Veritatis gaudium'* App. 2. https://www.vatican.va/content/francesco/en/apost_constitutions/documents/papa-francesco_costituzione-ap_20171208_veritatis-gaudium.html.

105 Pope Francis, Enc., *'Fratelli tutti'* 3. III. 2020. n. 3. 257. https://www.vatican.va/content/francesco/it/encyclicals/documents/papa-francesco_20201003_enciclica-fratelli tutti.

106 Ibid. n. 22.

107 Pope Francis' message on the 50th Day of Peace. 'Address of his Holiness Pope Francis to Participants in the International Symposium "Prospects for a World Free of Nuclear Weapons and for Integral Disarmament' https://w2.vatican.va/content/francesco/en/speeches/2017/november/documents/papa-francesco_20171110_convegno-disarmointegrale.html Pope Francis' speech at Hiroshima is especially poignant this field. https://www.npr.org/2019/11/24/782450610/pope-francis-in-visit-to-hiroshima-says-possession-of-nuclear-weapons-is-immoral?t=1632386455662. 'Pope, UN urge protection of environment in armed conflicts' https://www.vaticannews.va/en/world/news/2017-11/pope--un-urge-protection-of-environment-in-armed-conflicts-.html See also Christiansen Drew, 'The Church Says 'No' to Nuclear Weapons Pastoral and moral implications' (2017 English Edition) *La Civilta Cattolica* 3.

these classical lines of reasoning to justify their pre-emptive military strikes or operations. For this reason, amplified by the presence of extremely dangerous new military technologies, which threaten the future of mankind and nature alike, the classical arguments for a just war, as established by Saint Augustine, no longer apply. The Pope relies heavily on religious people, regardless of their religious affiliation, on global social and security issues. And in defending the created world, he takes the approach that it is a common home for all of us, again without denominational affiliation.[108] In summary, *Fratelli tutti* is the first papal document to provide a complex framework that is built upon the protection of the ecology and complete nuclear disarmament. Despite its novel approach, in formulating it, Pope Francis always draws on the works of his predecessors, which suggests that, due to the destructive nature of modern warfare, twentieth-century popes also had their doubts about the admissibility of the just war tradition.[109] At the same time, there has been much criticism of the Pope's position on just war tradition. Many have argued that this is not only inconsistent with the Church's tradition, but also with its current ethical teaching on war.[110] The defence of the innocent, of the homeland, of self-defence can create circumstances in which the use of military force is just. At the same time, the recent war in Europe seems to be prompting the Pope to rethink his critique of the just war tradition. Pope Francis' ethics of war is well summarised by Joe Capizzi in the light of the encyclic Fratelli tutti. The just war tradition really needs to be rethought. The Pope's anti-war and anti violence stance is clear. But he is also taking a moral stance on the current armed conflicts, and he takes into account the classical ethical categories of the just war, even if he does not state them explicitly.[111] This has been particularly underlined in the context of the Russian-Ukraine conflict.

108 Genc Mustaf, 'Fratelli Tutti: An Interpretation of Dialogue and Friendship in Society: An Islamic Perspective' 5. (2021) *The Journal of social encounters* 33–36.

109 John Sniegocki, 'Pope Francis, Fratelli Tutti, the Death Penalty, and War' 5 (2021) *The Journal of Social Encounters* 23–32.

110 Charles Russo, 'Pope Francis, Just War Theory, the Ukraine, and Beyond: Can War Be Just?' *Canopy Forum – On the Interactions of Law &* Religion https://canopyforum.org/2022/05/04/pope-francis-just-war-theory-the-ukraine-and-beyond-can-war-be-just/.

111 Mark Tooley and Joseph E. Capizzi, 'Joe Capizzi on Pope Francis & Just War' https://providencemag.com/video/joe-capizzi-on-pope-francis-just-war/.

6 Summary

As early as the fourth century, the Catholic Church was forced to express its ethical stance on war, which is a basic feature of our human existence. The rules which regulate how Christians should fight and/or go to war were defined by Saint Augustine. However, his guidelines never became a closed system because he left open the possibility that the appearance of new kinds of armaments, conflicts or actions might redefine the whole framework. The protection of nature was a late addition to this system. It was the often irreversible harm caused by modern weapons systems or military practices which made the theoreticians of the just war theory and the Catholic Church consider the ecological issue of this problem. Furthermore, we must not deny that the protection of the environment has never been an important issue within Western military thinking. This fact is quite succinctly expressed by Carl von Clausewitz when he argues that in war "both sides are committed to using as much force as necessary, without any limitations, so they may defeat their enemies."[112] This phrase is a great summary of Western military thinking. However, this type of thinking is incompatible with the protection of nature. Even so, armed forces have begun to reconsider their social role and the tasks they have to carry out in our modern societies. This includes the development of civil-military cooperation and non-combat related deployments. Nevertheless, one element is still missing: to accept the importance of environmental issues during military activities. Therefore, despite the presence of international or institutional guidance, combatants do not care much about the environment when they are carrying out military operations.[113] Pope Francis was the first pontiff to go beyond this by arguing that, within the Christian ethics of war, no war can be called just. Instead, only peace can be just. Pope Francis reached this conclusion after contrasting the issues of environmental damage, the power of modern nuclear weapons and the absurdity of poverty with the just war theory. The current pontiff concludes that, instead of adapting the just war theory to our contemporary challenges, we must put an end to the 1500-year-old Christian effort of trying to identify those circumstances and characteristics under which a war may be just. However, the Pope himself also uses elements of the just war tradition: self-defence, defence of others. In the context of the Ukrainian-Russian war, he drew attention to the duty to defend the homeland. Thus, Pope Francis' merit lies rather in the fact that he illustrates the evaluation of war in the most

112 Carl von Clausewitz ibid. (3. sec. 14).

113 Merrit Drucker, 'The military commander's responsibility for the environment' 11 (1989) *Environmental Ethics*, 135–152.

complex way possible, placing it in the context of the Church's social teaching as a whole. He points out how modern wars can have social repercussions that go beyond themselves, sometimes global, and how difficult-to-control economic interests can lie behind them. It is therefore difficult to speak today of just wars, to which we can add the serious environmental damage caused by modern wars. However, the Pope also emphasises the need to use force. He seems to be developing his own ethic of war, which incorporates elements of the classical just war tradition, even if he criticises the tradition itself.

Moreover, military activities still look anthropocentric, which means that the protection of human life is more important than the protection of the environment. However, people who adopt this human-centric worldview can also accept that pollution caused by military actions or personnel can harm the lives, health or livelihoods of other human beings. Thus, if we destroy the environment, we will also destroy human lives.[114] Several scholars have tried hard to adapt the just war tradition to the realities of ecology. However, these efforts are not especially convincing in light of the ecological damage caused by modern weapon systems. We must move beyond merely making this claim. Just as the Church spent centuries setting up the philosophical and theological underpinnings of the just war theory, now it is time for the Church to do the same for the theory of new military approach. We can only achieve this goal if we follow the transdisciplinary method recommended by Pope Francis' apostolic constitution *Veritatis Gaudium*. The theory must not only be supported by theological arguments but we must also use the findings and methodologies of military sciences, security studies, law, state studies and other related sciences.

---

114 Karl Mathiesen, 'What's the environmental impact of modern war?' *The Guardian* https://www.theguardian.com/environment/2014/nov/06/whats-the-environmental-impact-of-modern-war.

Index

If you have any questions regarding this title, please contact:

Koninklijke Brill BV
Plantijnstraat 2
2321 JC Leiden
Email: info@brill.com

Batch number: 10703839